The strategy of takeovers

A casebook of international practice

THE STRATEGY OF TAKEOVERS

A casebook of international practice

Anthony Vice

London · New York · St Louis · San Francisco · Düsseldorf
Johannesburg · Kuala Lumpur · Mexico · Montreal · New Delhi
Panama · Rio de Janeiro · Singapore · Sydney · Toronto

Published by

McGraw-Hill Book Company (UK) Limited

MAIDENHEAD BERKSHIRE ENGLAND

07 094235 8

PRINTED AND BOUND IN GREAT BRITAIN

Contents

For Elizabeth, Susan, John, and Philippa

Acknowledgements

I should like to acknowledge the help and advice of many busy executives. I am particularly grateful to James Slater; George Taylor; Sir Arnold Weinstock; Lord Stokes; Don Ryder; Lord Watkinson; John Read; Robert Clark; Derek Willis; M. Georges-Picot and Saul Steinberg.

The chapter on BSN was inspired by my old friend Michel Gabrysiak's book *Saint-Gobain-BSN* and is also based on *BSN contre Saint-Gobain* by B. Hartemann and R. Ducousset. My late colleague, Patricia Lloyd-Jones, wrote the chapter on Badische Anilin and Wintershall; it reflects her great knowledge of German business and public affairs.

This book was written while I was Editor of *The Times Business News*.

A.V.

Preface

Takeovers and mergers represent one of the most striking features of company growth. In this book I have analysed case studies involving nine recent mergers. In some, such as the alliance between Schweppes and Cadbury and Jim Slater's takeover of Forestal Land, much of the material has not been made public before; in the three overseas takeovers, Saint-Gobain, Badische Anilin and Wintershall, and Leasco-Chemical Bank, relatively little has been published in this country; in large, well documented takeovers, such as GEC's bids for AEI and English Electric, Reed-IPC, and Leyland-British Motor, I have tried to illustrate the corporate strategy which lay behind the specific headline-making moves. For this information, my acknowledgement to busy chairmen and chief executives of large companies is very real; the shortcomings in the analysis are wholly my own.

Through fluctuations in fashions of thinking, mergers are credited either with too great or too little importance. Probably the best guide lies in Gerald Newbould's estimate, expressed in his book *Management and Merger Activity*, that mergers in Britain involved some £5200 million in 1967–68. That is equivalent to two-thirds of all capital investment by the private sector in those years and to very nearly twice the amount of capital investment carried out by manufacturing industry alone. In other words, mergers in Britain are of major importance for industrial development. One problem, incidentally, lies in the use of terminology in that takeover, by contrast to merger, seems to carry undesirable overtones. Both terms centre on the acquisition of voting capital, in the formal sense of more than 50 per cent, in a company. Merger generally refers to an agreed transaction between two units of broadly comparable size, whereas takeover applies to a successful offer which was resisted by the 'victim's' board of directors, or more frequently, to the acquisition of a relatively small unit by a large one. If a distinction is to be made, it seems fair to say that GEC took over AEI, but later merged with English Electric.

Mergers are not, of course, new; they are at least as old as the joint-stock principle. The first great wave of merger activity originated in the United States, with battles for control of the railroads in the late nineteenth century.

This was followed by the creation of the Standard Oil Trust, probably the classic case of the use of mergers to create a monopoly situation which was eventually frustrated by the US Department of Justice. After Rockefeller, J. P. Morgan built up US Steel which escaped anti-trust action. In Britain, the proliferation of railway building brought a rash of mergers to maintain profitability; a similar trend developed in shipping, though the most ambitious merger group, Royal Mail, had to be reshaped after the slump of 1929 to 1931. The other feature of 1900 to 1930 was the internationalization of business, above all in the new industries. While the creation of Imperial Tobacco and British-American Tobacco attracted attention before 1914, other leading mergers included ICI, Royal Dutch-Shell, and Unilever.

The 'thirties produced a new kind of merger, the defensive merger, whose aim was to eliminate surplus production capacity and, if possible, create a company worth more, in stock exchange terms, than the sum of its parts. Cotton, shipping, and shipbuilding were among the first to be rationalized (an interwar term). The exponents of rationalization included Clarence Hatry, while it was later extended by government support.

Undervalued Assets

After the Second World War, mergers in Britain revived in yet another form. Many companies' assets, especially in property, had become undervalued, while stock exchange prices were also held down by government restraint on dividends. The result was a series of takeovers by enterprising bidders. Charles Clore's bid for Freeman, Hardy and Willis was probably the most famous of these, while Sir Isaac Wolfson and the late Lord Fraser were also noted practitioners. This period has been described by George Bull and myself in *Bid for Power*, published in 1958.

But the general undervaluation of companies inevitably disappeared, though Jim Slater was later to show that a skilful eye can still find attractive situations. The well known takeovers of the late 'fifties and 'sixties tended to centre on rival industrial strategies rather than financial situations, as shown in the epic battle for British Aluminium and the struggle for Odhams. Ironically, perhaps, it was one of Mr Clore's major forays, the attempt to take over Watney Mann, which inspired the City's first takeover code, published in 1959, and which in turn led to the creation of the present Takeover Panel.

The code reflected growing public awareness of the importance of mergers and takeovers, coupled with the belief in the City and industry that control by statute (in the way that President Roosevelt had created the Securities and Exchange Commission) was probably impracticable and certainly undesirable. Acting on this view, which was supported even by the Wilson Government, the City made substantial progress in evolving a code of fair treatment and fuller disclosure.

As the chapters on GEC and British Leyland show, the merger movement was also assisted by the creation of the Industrial Reorganization Corporation, set up in 1966 by the Labour Government and wound up by Mr Heath in 1970. The IRC deserves its own full history, but one indirect result of its activities was to highlight the widespread schizophrenia about takeovers, especially in the left-wing administration. On the one hand, mergers were extolled for improving Britain's competitive position against large US and European groups and for speeding up technological development; on the other hand, they were criticized for creating redundancies and dislocation, and for reflecting a profit-orientated capitalist society. This conflict was never fully resolved by the Wilson Government from 1964 to 1970.

All this merger activity, and the public interest which it has aroused, have created what seems to me a fundamental imbalance: that shareholders are well informed if their directors choose to expand through the acquisition of another company, but relatively badly informed if the same money is used to build a new factory. Over the whole area of companies' use of resources, shareholders and the public are well informed if this happens to take the form of the acquisition of another corporate entity. The answer to this obvious anomaly is to make companies' use of resources, and probably their supply of resources, subject to the same requirements of disclosure. Financial disclosure of this kind was largely ignored by the 1967 Companies Act, but the systematic reporting of resource use may form part of new company legislation to be introduced by the Heath Government.

Institutional Attitudes

This anomaly over mergers arises essentially from the view that they represent some peculiar form of company activity. In one important sense, too much is often expected of mergers and takeovers; by contrast with the US, they have become, in Britain, the only way of carrying through major boardroom changes. When one reviews major companies which got into difficulties, such as AEI and BMC, the obvious question is why did their shareholders allow such a situation to develop? The answer is that, in general, the large investment institutions in Britain have avoided involvement in management; they take action only when management makes a controversial move in the field of financial policy – such as the old GEC's re-financing. It seems to me a major defect in the structure of corporate ownership that the large institutional shareholders have not been prepared to take positive action. For one thing, early action could have avoided large companies reaching a situation where a takeover was the only answer. A solution through a bid also assumes that another group will be willing to take over the ailing company on terms which can appeal to the bidder's shareholders. Supporters of mergers and takeovers underrate the difficulty of making a contested bid. Some of these problems emerged in GEC's bid for AEI and in Electric and Musical's takeover of Associated British Picture Corporation. Moreover, one should not underestimate the powers of an established board to resist an unwanted, even though well founded, takeover. Most of these examples never become public; but there are many cases of the skill of an established board in fighting off an unwanted bidder, for example, the Savoy Hotel in Britain (described in *Bid for Power*), Saint-Gobain in France, and Chemical Bank in the US.

In many cases, a bid may not be the answer to a company's problems; what is often needed is a solution to particular management difficulties. Added to these obstacles are the periodic doubts, unresolved and possibly unresolvable, about the relation of company size to economic efficiency. To the extent that these doubts are well founded, a merger may not only fail to solve a company's problems, but could even generate a fresh set of difficulties.

Two conclusions emerge from recent takeovers in Britain. One is that the Takeover Panel, in its new form under Lord Shawcross and Ian Fraser, has proved a considerable success. It has shown that self-regulation can be more effective, as well as being inherently more desirable, than statutory control. The next step could, and in my view should, be the widening of the Panel's scope to include any change in the effective control of a company. In other words, the scope of takeovers should be widened to correspond to company practice and include effective as well as legal control. In Britain, by contrast with the US, a takeover has become defined as covering more than 50 per cent of all votes; but in many cases effective control, especially in the sense of a blocking vote, can lie with a smaller holding, 10 per cent or more, particularly if the other holdings are widely spread.

The other conclusion is that disclosure of company activities should be made more systematic – by applying merger criteria to all uses of resources. Shareholders should expect to be given full details of all resource uses which involve say more than 5 per cent of total assets, whether or not these are accomplished through another corporate entity – what the world knows as mergers and takeover bids.

Anthony Vice

Foreword

Mergers and acquisitions have always formed part of the restructuring process by which the economy initiates and responds to change. As Anthony Vice indicates, however, the scale which the acquisition movement has attained in recent years makes it an outstanding feature of the postwar industrial world. The movement began to gather pace in the early 'fifties, when share prices were relatively low in relation to asset values and when many of the companies taken over were attractive for their liquidity. In this period, purely financial factors played an important role in the acquisitive motive. In the 'sixties, on the other hand, the undervaluation of share prices disappeared, and so did spare company liquidity; the driving forces behind the takeover and merger process were now largely commercial, although undoubtedly complex in character.

At the same time, by any standard the scale of this activity increased. In the 'fifties less than 10 per cent of the total uses of quoted company funds went on acquisitions. Between 1960 and 1965, this figure averaged 16 per cent. After a brief fall in 1966, when share prices declined, there developed a veritable merger boom, culminating in 1968, when the proportion of the total flow of company funds devoted to acquisitions reached the unprecedented figure of about one-third. There was hardly a large quoted company that did not become involved in the widespread reshuffle of industrial ownership, on one side or the other. In the late 'sixties, the movement had clearly become cumulative, as company after company sought to protect its industrial position against the actual or potential increase in the share of an industry's assets passing into the hands of its competitors. The desire to increase or protect one's market share seems to have been the most prevalent of the many forces at work; most mergers and acquisitions have apparently been 'horizontal' in character.

The scale of the acquisition movement during the past decade contrasts sharply with the extent of informed inquiry into the exact balance of forces in operation, the degree of success or failure of the process, or the implications for public policy of the movement as a whole. Such as it is, the available literature on the process, in the US as well as in this country, suggests that most takeovers and mergers have not produced much net benefit to the share-holders of the acquiring company, who on average have had to pay about one-third more than the pre-bid price of the company being absorbed in order to carry out the bid. Where the bid has been opposed, the premium on the pre-bid price has usually been higher, especially where a battle has developed between rival suitors. In this latter case especially, the evidence suggests that the price eventually paid has reflected, not only the increase in profits expected over time, but also the *loss* of profits feared in the event of the bid being lost to a rival. This is understandable, but it undoubtedly strengthens the temptation to pay too much.

There are indeed *prima facie* grounds suggesting that in many cases the successful bidder begins his marriage, whether in the form of willing merger or contended suit, with the scales tipped against him. Organic resistance to transplants seems to apply to the industrial as well as to the human body; there are many forms of 'counter-surgery' to overcome. Differences in control systems and even in forms of aspiration and motivation have to be resolved. Making mergers work is not just a question of rationalizing production facilities; but this alone is difficult enough when large scale redundancies are involved. Neither is it merely a matter of reaping the semi-monopolistic gains of increased market concentration, gains which in turn may prove to be disappointingly small because of the development of some form of countervailing power, or of the growth of imports, or indeed because of government policy.

Gains to profit margins may well accrue from a more economical product pattern, concentration on the most efficient plant structure, or from a stronger hold on the market; but against these must be set at least two forms of cost. One is in the form of the diversion of scarce managerial time and energy to making the merger or acquisition succeed. This task must be given to the most talented and energetic of a group's executives; and it is one that usually takes longer than is expected. If the will to take unpopular action does not exist, or if its implementation is delayed, the potential benefits of a merger are correspondingly harder to obtain; and investors who have paid a high price for their acquisition do not have unlimited patience. Where a weak company is taken over, its problems usually turn out to be even more profound than had been appreciated.

A second source of cost is the tendency for wage and salary levels, in-cluding such matters as pension rights, to be 'levelled up' within the newly formed group. Perhaps union pressure would eventually have brought about a similar result as far as the operatives of two separate firms are concerned, but the process is undoubtedly accelerated by a merger, which also tends to carry the trend to managerial levels where such pressures might otherwise be much weaker.

Reflections such as these arise from common observation and from the literature on the results of mergers and takeovers. It is, however, too easy to generalize. Every acquisition or merger situation has its own characteristics, in terms of its industrial setting, the strengths and weaknesses of the companies involved and the qualities of the leading human characters in what is often an exciting drama.

Anthony Vice's book is particularly welcome in that it fills one of the gaps in the literature. By presenting a close study of the events leading to a number of merger situations, it enables us to understand more fully the subsequent history of the marriage.

Mr Vice's book makes abundantly clear the variety of merger situations, especially in terms of the pressures that lead a large company to feel that a particular acquisition is desirable. Perhaps making acquisitions is itself a special kind of business, calling for the exercise of rare skills if it is to be successful. But there is a world of difference between the conglomerate acquisition by companies such as Slater Walker, where the bidder makes a deliberate and relatively free choice from a comparatively wide range of tempting situations, and the case where a company feels almost compelled to make a particular acquisition because of a dangerous situation that has developed inside its industry or because of its own internal needs. Not the least merit of Mr Vice's studies is that they highlight the difference between the factors at work in individual merger situations. This book is one about people. For statistics and economic generalizations cannot by themselves provide that texture and colour of a merger situation that give it life. Whether a bid is successfully, and often surprisingly, contested, as in the two Continental case histories described here, or whether it goes through, it is in the last resort the personal qualities of the individuals concerned that decide whether the potential benefits of an industrial marriage, no less than in ordinary life, are brought to fruition.

Harold Rose,
Esmee Fairbarn Professor of Finance,
London Graduate School of Business Studies.

How Jim Slater Bought Forestal

Jim Slater has become a byword in Britain for a new type of corporate activity: the ability to take over a company and then so to reorganize its management and trading activities, by selling off some assets and redeploying others, that the market value of the company is greatly increased. Many other groups have tried to imitate the Slater technique of buying companies, reshaping their assets, and emerging with a substantial profit; but none of Slater's imitators has experienced anything like the success on anything like his scale. To draw any kind of parallel, one must go back to the early 'fifties and Mr Clore's takeover of Freeman, Hardy and Willis. To set out the full story of Slater Walker's development would take a book in itself. Possibly the best way of showing the Slater technique is to describe the acquisition of Forestal Land and Timber, an old established merchandising and commodity group based in South America. Slater Walker paid £10·5 million for Forestal, which was disposed of for £18·4 million, giving Slater a profit £7·9 million and terms which the Forestal directors could recommend.

Staggering Growth

By any standards, Slater's growth has been staggering. As recently as 1964, Slater bought control of a property company called H. Lotery. He put into it £25 000 of his own money, borrowing another £325 000 from various banks, giving him £350 000 altogether. He also assembled a syndicate of friends and associates, including the banks, to put up a further £350 000, and with the total £700 000 bought 49 per cent of the company which was then valued at a total of £1·4 million. Lotery's name was changed to Slater Walker Securities, which forms the base of the present group. From £1·4 million, by internal expansion and acquisitions, the group had grown by late 1970 to more than £70 million.

Jim Slater left school when he was sixteen, was articled to a firm of accountants, and qualified at twenty-four. He spent five years with a firm of accountants called Croydon and King in Victoria, and a final year with Cooper Brothers, one of the leading City firms.

His first industrial job was with a company called Dohm Limited, run

1

by a Danish financier of the same name. As a result of internal dissension, Slater found himself general manager after only three months. Dohm then appointed Slater manager of his other subsidiaries and Slater went through the group as a trouble-shooter. When Dohm's son was about to join the business, Slater left, and became secretary of Park Royal Vehicles, then a subsidiary of the Associated Commercial Vehicles group. One useful piece of experience, after Slater had been there two years, was the twelve months he spent closing down Crossley Motors, a subsidiary in Manchester. Slater then became commercial director of AEC, the largest subsidiary in the ACV group, and held this job when Leyland took over. Slater became commerical manager of the Leyland group, which also included Triumph, Albion, and Scammel. After about a year, he was made deputy to Donald Stokes in his capacity as Sales Director. Stokes was also chief executive with Sir William Black as chairman.

Jim Slater had established an outstandingly successful industrial career and had acquired a range of useful managerial experience. Slater had begun to take a serious interest in the stock market just before the Leyland take-over of ACV. Between the ages of thirty-two and thirty-five (when he left Leyland), Slater turned his modest £2000 of savings into £50000. Slater relied heavily on borrowing: against his original savings of £2000 he borrowed £8000. Slater multiplied his capital a total of twenty-five times by seeking companies, generally smaller ones, which were ripe for a 'status change', a term coined by Slater. His technique was to invest in growth stocks which had a good record, looked like having a good future, enjoyed a reasonably strong cash position, and were selling on an unusually high price-earnings yield – or a low price-earnings ratio. Slater explained the two-fold benefit from successful investment in this way: when the company reported its next year's improved earnings not only did the shares go up with the higher profits, they also went up because the market gave the shares a high growth status expressed through a higher price-earnings ratio.

When H. Lotery became Slater Walker Securities in 1964, Slater launched a series of acquisitions buying about a score of public companies. Slater Walker became one of the first industrial conglomerates.

The new era began quietly with the 1964 accounts showing £155000 for advisory services and finance companies. The following year, Beaufort House, the main property asset, was sold for £1·85 million, while advisory services and other income had produced £94000. The pace began to increase in 1966. In July, Slater Walker Securities merged their banking business in a new company with Rosenthal and Partners and during the same month put in a bid for Thomas Brown. This first bid was in many ways a pointer to the future. The *Investors Chronicle* wrote:

> If ever there was an outstanding case of a company with assets not earning their keep it is difficult to pin-point a finer example than that of Thomas

2

Brown, which carried on business as general merchants and manufacturers in Australia.

Slater's next major deal, in October 1966, was to gain full control of the Slater Walker Industrial group, which owned substantial interests in Productofoam Holdings and George Wilson Gas Meters. In January 1967, Slater launched a bid for Greengate and Irwell Rubber, in which a 16 per cent holding had been built up. (A detailed analysis, by C. F. Pratten, of the results of this takeover appeared in *Moorgate and Wall Street* of Spring 1970.) Slater's accounts in May 1967 showed that Thomas Brown's assets of £2·25 million had been acquired for £1·35 million. The loss-making wholesale side had been closed down and about £900 000 was reckoned to have been raised from the sale of assets. That same year, Slater launched six other major acquisitions; the remaining shares in Productofoam Holdings and George Wilson, Constructors, Newmans Holdings, Kirby Holdings, Kirby Brothers, and Nathaniel Lloyd.

The following year, 1968, saw a series of further deals, notably the acquisition of Crittall-Hope, makers of metal windows, Keith Blackman (one of the less successful bids), a tie-up with James Hanson's Wiles Group, and most important of all, the takeover of Sir Isaac Wolfson's Drage's complex of industrial and banking interests. The Drage's deal was of crucial strategic importance to Slater, as it moved him away from industrial development into banking and finance where Slater himself saw the most appealing growth possibilities. Then, in the early days of 1969, came the £10 million plus offer for the Forestal Land, Timber and Railways Company Limited.

How Forestal Grew

Forestal was originally made public back in 1906, sponsored by the well known financier Baron Emile D'Erlanger, who was chairman of Forestal for many years. Forestal grew in the tradition of British based international merchandising groups. It boasted a prestigious board including some eminent Continental merchants. In the years leading to the First World War, Forestal raised money to expand in Argentina and North America. Its business was the production and preparation of quebracho extract from the quebracho tree, a natural extract used in the preparation of heavy leather. In a statement to doubtless proud shareholders in 1913, the directors revealed that the company controlled nearly 5 million acres of land in Argentina, along with half a dozen factories and some 200 miles of railway; it had also taken over land and buildings in Brooklyn, New York, through the acquisition of the New York Tanning and Extract Company. During these years, Forestal maintained its boardroom links with other international commodity groups since both the Earl of Selbourne and Lord Luke were directors. Forestal survived the depression and even managed to raise fresh capital

3

in 1934, thanks no doubt to its powerful backers. Ordinary shareholders went without any dividend from 1931 to 1934, but the preference payment was regularly met – overall, not a bad performance. Forestal, like many other worldwide commodity producers, recovered slowly during the 'thirties and early 'forties, but the board decided that the company should spread its interests. Tanning relied on three raw materials: quebracho from South America, mimosa or wattle from Africa, and chestnut from Europe. Forestal decided to move into the African wattle industry, a development that was not immediately successful and which brought about some board changes, but ultimately paid off handsomely. One of the men who became a director of Forestal around this time was George Taylor, later a deputy chairman of the powerful Bank of London and South America and who, as chairman of Forestal in 1969, agreed to the bid from Slater.

But Forestal's entire world, along with that of many smaller producers, was about to fall apart. In 1948 came the invention of synthetic leather, which greatly reduced the demand for natural heavy leather and, therefore, for the vegetable tanning process on which Forestal depended. The full importance of the synthetic leather and the effect of its growing use on the demand for heavy leather and so for vegetable tanning extracts did not emerge until the mid 'fifties, after the end of the Korean War. What happened to the vegetable tanning extract industry across the world represents a textbook case of a commodity faced by a massive and permanent contraction in demand, yet unable to reduce production over the short term. George Taylor, who succeeded Sir Gerard d'Erlanger as chairman of Forestal in 1962 (Sir Gerard was the son of Emile d'Erlanger, Forestal's founder-chairman), set out the situation: the wattle industry in South and East Africa, which had expanded rapidly after the Second World War, owned plantations designed to yield about 180 000 tons with a factory capacity of 200 000 tons. The quebracho industry in South America, which had shipped 176 000 tons in 1955, the last normal year for the industry, had a factory capacity of 320 000 tons and virtually unlimited supplies from standing forests. The chestnut industry, with annual shipments of 80 000 to 90 000, had a factory capacity about twice that size. Against this massive output, capacity demand had fallen below 400 000 tons by 1960 and was still declining.

The immediate effect of this position, predictably enough, was chronic price instability and occasional price wars. The Forestal board decided to tackle this problem in two ways: first, to secure international co-operation which would contain the fall in extract prices; and second, to diversify Forestal's own business.

From 1955 to 1963 the Forestal directors, with the help of the Argentinian and Paraguayan governments and those of South Africa, Rhodesia, and Kenya, struggled to obtain co-operation and rationalization. Thanks to support from all the governments concerned, a large measure of rationalization was

4

achieved in the wattle and quebracho industries, so that the price war of 1960–61 was the last splutter in the struggle.

By 1963, the Forestal directors could be well pleased that they had played a major part in securing stability in world markets for vegetable tanning extracts, but the long term outlook remained bleak: the best that they and other producers could hope for was stable selling prices. This meant that profits would be slowly eroded by rising production costs. Moreover, if there were further improvements or new discoveries in synthetics, leading to a further serious contraction in the overall market, then Forestal's basic business could well cease to be profitable. Vegetable tanning extracts, depending on the natural heavy leather market, could go the way of natural dyes after the invention of synthetic substitutes in the late nineteenth century.

Diversification Plans

To meet this possibility, and to use shareholders' funds profitably, Forestal had started to diversify in 1957. The centre of its diversification programme was in Britain, where planning for new businesses began in the middle 'fifties. A development unit was set up to exploit existing ideas. Forestal also moved into new fields, buying Cruickshank, the metal platers, Grindley, makers of paint driers, V. W. Eves, manufacturers of animal feeding stuffs, and several others. Forestal's diversification schemes proved more successful than many others, mainly because the board aimed either at development based on the existing Ditton, Liverpool, unit, or at the purchase of companies to be maintained as going concerns. Thus, some of the chemicals made by Eves were produced at Ditton, and Grindley products were merged with Ditton's chemical manufacturing. By 1962, Forestal had put £1·5 million into its new companies, though large overheads wiped out profits. Losses were made, mainly because re-location costs proved unexpectedly high, leading to a deficit of £222000 in 1962–63. But from 1964 onwards, Forestal's new British business prospered. Eves was sold at a large profit, and Forestal moved into the health foods business. Cruickshank grew, and the chemical side specialized successfully in water treatment, under licence from a US group.

Forestal directors handled the diversification programme with considerable skill (as the disposals after the Slater takeover were to show), but they faced a fundamental strategic problem. The companies which Forestal had built up were small to medium sized concerns which probably had no long term future as independent units. Their development posed problems for Forestal. The move into health foods called for the acquisition of shops to support the manufacturing processes, but Forestal's funds were limited. What, then, was the long term future? Forestal's vegetable tanning business was bound to decline slowly, especially as Argentina was suffering from

5

currency depreciation which steadily reduced the sterling value of Forestal's profits and assets. The industrial side was basically too small and would take many years to develop from its own resources. Forestal could have continued to buy and sell industrial companies, in effect turning into a miniature Slater Walker, but the board decided, reasonably enough, that this would represent too great a departure in policy and management.

By the late 'sixties, it was beginning to be apparent that a takeover was the inevitable, indeed the desirable, ultimate aim for the company. There was the probability that one of the US international groups might make an offer in order to exploit Forestal's interests in Africa and South America. The directors kept in touch informally with one of the leading New York banks, but no approaches came. Their obvious alternative policy was to set about liquidating the company, but in Forestal's position this would have posed great difficulties. For one thing, the group was spread across the world with subsidiaries operating under a variety of different laws and systems of exchange control. Second, Forestal held a dominant position in the vegetable extract business, so that the mere announcement of its proposed liquidation would have made a sale more difficult. Then along came Jim Slater.

It was in the autumn of 1968 that the Forestal board first heard suggestions that Slater might be interested; until then, a takeover of £10 million plus would have been no easy matter for Slater Walker. One path which led Slater to Forestal was Barrow, Hepburn and Gale, a large tanning and leather business in which Slater Walker had built up a 30 per cent holding and which had trading associations with Forestal. Slater also commissioned independent reports from Africa and Argentina: both these areas could have presented realization problems, but Slater was already talking to 'Tiny' Rowland's Lonrho group in Africa, while from Argentina it was suggested that a local consortium might be interested.

When Slater approached the Forestal board, they were, as has been explained, prepared to discuss an offer. For them, a sale to Slater would represent handing over the business to a professional disposer of companies, as opposed to trying to do the job themselves. To fix a price, the board had two questions to answer: what was Forestal worth, and how large a discount should they accept as, in effect, a liquidation fee for Slater Walker? While the talks were going on, rumours began to fly in the stock exchange. Forestal's price had started to edge up, possibly because Slater Walker had been building up a holding. (By the time of the formal offer to shareholders, at the end of January 1969, Slater Walker owned 480 000 ordinary and 150 000 preference shares in Forestal.) The obvious attraction of Forestal for speculators was that each of the 5·6 million ordinary shares was worth £2·75 in balance sheet values – well above any recent or prospective share price in the stock market.

6

Shares Leap

On Thursday, 9 January, Forestal shares leaped 30p from £1·02½ to £1·32½ in the face of 'No comment' from Slater Walker. The following day, the Forestal board publicly announced that 'preliminary discussions' were taking place with Slater Walker, though the statement added that these discussions 'are at this stage tentative only'. But there was no stopping the speculators: Forestal shares jumped another 35p to £1·67½. Taylor was even compelled formally to deny reports that £2·75 represented a 'considerable understatement' of the true asset value. Just how much was Forestal worth? This question, which intrigued dealers in the City, represented the key problem for Forestal directors and their advisers, Schroders. The starting point had to be the balance sheet, which showed £2·75 a share, or a total value of just over £15 million. But two of Forestal's businesses were greatly overpriced: the Argentine interests, which had been carried in the books for many years at their cost price of £5·01 million were clearly worth less. In 1967, the Argentine produced only gross dividends of £173 000 and retained profits worth another £50 000 at prevailing exchange rates. Forestal's other overstated asset was the business in Rhodesia and Kenya, on which so much money had been spent towards the end of the Second World War. These companies stood in the books at £4·5 million, but were reckoned by the board to be worth no more than £2 million, which proved to be an extremely accurate forecast.

In these two sectors, therefore, Forestal's assets were worth £4 million to £4·5 million less than the book value. But against this, some interests were worth more than their balance sheet valuation. The South African company, standing in the balance sheet at £3·5 million, was thought to be worth between £6 million and £7 million. This was a major attraction for Slater Walker. In Britain, diversification had succeeded so well, that the industrial companies, shown at £1·5 million were estimated to be worth at least twice that. The upshot of these calculations, after allowing for investments and other assets, was that Forestal at current values was worth rather more than £14 million, equal to £1 million below the balance sheet total and representing between £2 and £2·25 a share.

What discount should the Forestal directors accept on this asset value? They and their advisers took the view that a 10 per cent discount would have been normal, but given the particular problems of Forestal, the nature and geographical spread of its business, about 20 per cent would be reasonable. Agreement was reached, and on 31 January, N. M. Rothschild, acting for Slater Walker, sent out the formal offer to Forestal shareholders. The basic Slater offer was almost wholly in shares (two Slater Walker shares plus 75p cash for every five units in Forestal), but there was an all cash option of £1·65. Preference shareholders were offered £1 cash for shares which had been selling at 75p. Though some recent buyers of the shares may have been disappointed, this price compared with the £1 at which Forestal shares were standing before the bid rumours broke. The Slater Walker offer closed in late February and by the middle of March the bidder was assured of 100 per cent control. Forestal shareholders had found the offer appealing, though their reaction had been hard to predict: the shares were widely spread with no single group owning as much as 5 per cent. The board's own holdings were nominal, less than 4000 units out of the total 5·6 million, and the large holdings which existed in Forestal's early years had long since been broken up. There were only three blocks of any significance: the Fontana family in Spain who had long standing associations with the company, and who had formerly been represented on the Forestal board; the Bemberg family in Argentina; and an anonymous Argentinian group which had apparently been formed to press for development of the South American properties.

Forestal's sixty years of independence came to an end, and Jim Slater and his colleagues started to do their sums in earnest. Forestal had cost Slater Walker a total of £10·5 million. Cash offered for the ordinary and preference shares totalled £6·68 million; Slater Walker had issued 1·22 million of its own shares, which were valued at £3 each, and so represented a further £3·67 million. The costs of the bid were £142000, which included investigations in South America and Africa, and also reflected assistance in Argentina.

Slater's two problem areas in realizing Forestal's business lay in Argentina and Africa. In East Africa, there were surplus cattle estates and stations, while the Rhodesian company, with book assets of just under £3 million, posed obvious difficulties for any British group. Slater was having talks with Lonrho on other African assets as part of a global package. Jim Slater and 'Tiny' Rowland met to work out the deal. Neither of them, it was said, had actually ever seen any wattle. The result was that the cattle farms and tanning extract businesses in East and Central Africa were sold to Lonrho for £2·5 million – again, close to the estimate made by the Forestal board. Slater took Lonrho shares, which were then standing at their peak. When Slater eventually sold these, the Lonrho shares had dropped more than £1 million; the credit from this deal finally stood in Slater's books at £1·35 million.

Disposing of Forestal's Argentinian interests proved a more complex business; but Slater Walker had the advantage of being able, to a large extent, to continue and complete a programme already initiated by Forestal. First, the group sold the land and city property, but not to a single buyer, as had been under negotiation, but piecemeal, in cash sales, to a number of buyers, spread over 1969 and 1970. The proceeds realized a useful £2·5 million. As the second part of the operation, it authorized the Forestal people to continue and complete the merging of the extract side in Argentina with similar French interests there, controlled by the Rhone Poulenc group.

This represented practically the final step in the rationalization of the Argentinian quebracho industry.

The new merged group, Unitan, came into operation on 1 January 1970 with Slater Walker owning 50 per cent of the capital. On the basis of 1969 profits and a modest price-earnings ratio, the value of the interest was estimated at approximately £2·5 million. In the final tidying-up operation on the extract side, Slater Walker set up Forestal International to act as distributor world wide for the tanning extract industry and to provide technical help and liaison between the various companies. Forestal International, it was estimated, would handle about 70 per cent of the world distribution of tanning materials. Based in London, it is owned jointly by a group which includes the South African wattle industry, Lonrho, the Commonwealth Development Corporation, and Argentinian interests. But before putting this company together, Slater Walker had released unused assets which realized £230 000 to add to the credit side of the deal.

At this point, then, Slater Walker had received, or anticipated receiving, £1·35 million for East Africa and Rhodesia, £2·5 million for estate sales in Argentina, and £230 000 from putting together Forestal International – a total of £4·1 million or over one-third of the entire cost of the bid. In addition, the investment in the Argentinian quebracho operation through Unitan was estimated to be worth £2·5 million.

British Assets

Before analysing the South African operation, which in many ways represented the heart of the transaction, it might be useful to see how Slater handled Forestal's British interests. In Britain, Forestal owned the three diversified companies operating in water treatment, metal coating, and health foods. None of these fitted with other companies inside the Slater Walker groups, so the decision was taken to sell them all. Forestal also held in Britain some miscellaneous assets and investments, which were marked down for sale. These other assets included, for instance, Forestal's head office in John Adam Street behind the Strand in London. Forestal's final board meeting was held there on 16 September 1969 followed by a formal annual general meeting two days later; from then on Forestal's London head office ceased to function.

The prices realized for Forestal's three diversified interests fully matched the Forestal's board's original forecasts and served to justify their programme over previous years. The chemical division, the largest of the three, already operated through its water treatment side as a licensee of the Dearborn chemical division of W. R. Grace and Co. Grace was, therefore, a natural buyer and the entire chemical side, which also included Farnell Carbons and Kaylene Chemicals, was sold to W. R. Grace, Inc for £1·5 million. Cruick-shanks, the smallest of the three units, which had been part of Forestal for more than ten years, was sold to M. & T. Chemicals Inc for £717 000. Forestal's health food side, operated by Alfonal and Heath and Heather (and whose wide ranging interests included the nutritional magazine, *Here's Health*), went to Booker McConnell for £1·13 million.

These three companies, therefore, produced £3·36 million. Slater Walker still had to dispose of a number of miscellaneous, though valuable, assets. These notably included Forestal's head office, which went to the Church Commissioners for £425 000; some surplus industrial properties were also sold for £332 000, of which land at Ditton brought £220 000. Forestal held various investments, which were disposed of for £190 000 along with some small companies which brought in another £40 000. Forestal controlled two companies in Germany, Gebruder Muller and Deutsch-Koloniale, which Slater Walker decided to retain in order to form the basis for Slater Walker Germany. These companies were valued at £350 000 having produced just 2 per cent of Forestal's 1967 profits, or around £15 000 a year.

All this, therefore, left Slater Walker with proceeds of £8·77 million plus the £2·5 million quebracho investment – £11·27 million overall, to set against the cost of £10·5 million. The crux of Slater's plans for Forestal lay in the disposal of the South African company, Natal Tanning Extract. This was easily the most important of Forestal's three African companies. The other two, East African Tanning Extract and Rhodesian Wattle, had been sold to Lonrho. These three companies produced 64 per cent of Forestal's entire profits in 1966 and 54 per cent in 1967 – a deterioration resulting mainly from a setback suffered by the Rhodesian company. The Forestal board and Schroders had valued Natal Tanning at between £6 million and £7 million, compared with a book value of £3·5 million. Could Slater Walker realize this sort of figure?

The South African Key

The key to Slater's operation lay in the use of Slater Walker Securities (South Africa). Slater Walker (South Africa) had been built up on lines similar to those of its parent in London. It enjoyed fast profit growth and, most important, an attractive price-earnings valuation. The magic was to put Natal Tanning, with its substantial assets and sizeable profits into Slater Walker (South Africa) and so valorize the former Forestal company on the same appealing basis as its new parent. In 1968 alone, the price of Slater Walker (South Africa) shares had soared on the Johannesburg Stock Exchange from R0·90 to R4·40. The injection of Natal added not merely to its own value, but also to that of Slater Walker (South Africa). Slater Walker had found themselves in South Africa through the acquisition of Crittall-Hope, the metal window manufacturers, in June 1968; that deal brought 69 per cent of a publicly quoted South African company, Crittall-Hope (South Africa). Slater then sold off the window manufacturing assets to Wire

Industries of South Africa for shares and cash, and launched on an aggressive takeover programme which brought the transformation of the share price. Slater Walker (South Africa) bought Standard Optical and acquired a stake in Abercom Investments which itself proved an outstanding stock market performer. Slater also injected into Slater Walker (South Africa) the Berg River Textile group of South Africa which had joined Slater Walker – as had Crittall-Hope – through the acquisition of its British parent, in this case Philips Brocklehurst which had formed part of the Drage's complex. Because of an eventually unsuccessful negotiation, this deal was delayed, but in July 1969 Slater Walker (South Africa) took over Natal Tanning Extract from Forestal. The terms, which were agreed by independent advisers, involved the issue of 1·5 million shares, which went, of course, to Slater Walker in London – representing a bid value of R11·25 million. Natal Tanning brought projected 1969 profits of R1·25 million and, more important, it contributed net tangible assets of R13 million. Slater Walker was able, in effect, to attach Slater Walker (South Africa) values to Natal Tanning while keeping a large block of shares which maintained its own holding in Slater Walker (South Africa) at around 75 per cent. By moving Natal Tanning Extract into Slater Walker (South Africa), the London company had, in effect, doubled Natal's value. Natal Tanning's profits, too, were moving smartly ahead from R767 000 in 1968 to R1·44 million, rather better than the original projection in 1969 and R1·67 million in 1970. Slater Walker valued the shares it had received for Natal Tanning at £7·13 million – slightly ahead even of the Forestal's board's estimate.

Adding this £7·13 million brought Slater Walker's total receipts for Forestal to a final £18·1 million against the cost of £10·5 million. Jim Slater could well justify the brief three-line statement in his annual report of 1969 concerning Forestal: '. . . we have disposed of many of this company's assets on very satisfactory terms.'

Forestal presents, in many ways, the classical features of a takeover. Forestal itself had lost its industrial base through the discovery of synthetic leather; despite the successful attempts at diversification, a takeover of the company was inevitable. Slater Walker could afford to bid for the company partly because disposal was its business, but principally because it had available two vehicles into which Forestal assets could be injected: Lonrho and, above all, Slater Walker (South Africa). Forestal directors were able to recommend a bid which gave shareholders a substantial profit on any recent or foreseeable stock market price; Slater Walker made a profit, part cash and part paper, of over £7 million. Such is the stuff of successful takeover bids.

GEC-AEI-EE

'Except between the twenty-first and the end of the month, when I'm going through the monthly reports, I'm not very busy really. I browse around a bit.' Thus spoke Sir Arnold Weinstock who, while still in his early forties, became chief executive of Britain's largest electrical complex, the result of the takeover by GEC of AEI and the subsequent merger with English Electric. Weinstock has also established in Britain an outstanding position as the exemplar of modern management. How does Weinstock work?

Weinstock's career falls into two clear phases. First, the middle and late 'sixties when, starting as a virtually unknown man, he transformed GEC from an ailing giant into a modern, successful company. The second phase, which is still under way, began in late 1967 with his successful, but strongly contested battle for control of AEI, which was followed by the merger, in the following year, with English Electric. By the end of 1968, Weinstock was chief executive of a group with annual sales approaching £1000 million, employing more than 200 000 people (the largest single employer of labour outside the nationalized industries), and responsible to a critical degree for the growth and future prosperity of Britain's electrical engineering industry.

Arnold Weinstock was born in 1924 of a Jewish family in North London. His father was a tailor, an immigrant from Poland, both parents died while Weinstock was young, and he was brought up by an elder brother. On leaving school, Weinstock went to the London School of Economics. He was evacuated during the Second World War to Cambridge, where he took a degree in statistics. He was called up in 1944 and spent three years as a junior administrative assistant in the Admiralty – quite happy, as he himself said later, on a salary of £420 a year and 'some subsidy' towards his living costs. When Weinstock was demobilized in 1947, he was introduced, through his elder brother, to Louis Scott, a West End estate agent who had established a reputation as a property dealer. Friends urged him to join Scott, with whom he worked for seven years, until 1954. By the time he left, Weinstock had built up unusual qualities. He had studied statistics, and even now must be one of the very few senior executives in British industry who is a Fellow of the Statistical Society. To this, he had added seven years of working for an entrepreneur whose prime aim was profitable deals. In 1949, while working for Scott, Weinstock married Netta, the younger daughter of Michael Sobell who, like Weinstock's father was an immigrant from Europe, and one of the pioneers in radio and television. Sobell later became well known for his large gifts to charity.

Weinstock joined Sobell in 1954, just after Sobell had re-established his business through an unusual deal. In the early 'fifties, Great Universal Stores placed a large order with EMI for a supply of its branded radios. EMI was fully occupied in meeting the postwar consumer boom, but offered to put its brand name on radios if GUS were agreeable to the production being sub-contracted to Sobell. GUS agreed, but EMI entered into a contract with Sobell of a longer term than their own principal contract with GUS. When government restrictions were imposed on consumer spending, GUS ended its contract with EMI, who then found itself with a substantial commitment to Sobell. This was finally resolved by EMI transferring back to Sobell the business which he had sold, while EMI kept the brand name.

Radio and Allied

This led to the creation of Radio and Allied Industries, which Arnold Weinstock joined as the proprietor's son-in-law at the age of thirty. Weinstock spent the years from 1954 onwards building up a thorough knowledge of the consumer electrical business, and establishing a formidable reputation in Allied itself and among its competitors and suppliers. Weinstock's rules were formalized by Kenneth Bond, four years Weinstock's senior, who was a former partner in Cooper and Cooper, the City accountants. Bond joined Weinstock in Radio and Allied in 1957, became a director of GEC in 1962, and is now its deputy managing director.

Weinstock instituted a thorough system of cost control which enabled Radio and Allied to undercut its established rivals. He also introduced new policies on the launching of new models and in 1956 acquired McMichael. Thanks largely to his efforts, Radio and Allied was able to go public showing profits of more than £1 million. Radio and Allied had a short career as an independent public company. Sobell and Weinstock realized that their success depended to an important extent on the expansion of one specific consumer product, while other groups in the electrical industry were also turning to rationalization. After a number of abortive talks, Sobell and Weinstock were introduced to Sir Arnold Lindley, who had taken over as chairman of GEC. Lindley's own electrical consumer side was losing money. He took the view that Radio and Allied's proved management could benefit GEC, while the terms of the deal brought a substantial increase in GEC's profits. The takeover of Radio and Allied by GEC was completed through a share exchange which left the Sobell and Weinstock families holding about 15 per cent of GEC's ordinary capital.

Weinstock and Sobell joined the main board of GEC, to which Sir Arnold Lindley himself had succeeded only a few months before. Lindley, an engineer, who had spent his working life with the company, took over at a particularly difficult time. GEC was the most consumer-oriented company by contrast with the two other major companies in the industry – AEI and English Electric. Like many other large companies, GEC had prospered by meeting the postwar boom in consumer demand, a boom which was prolonged, by contrast with the post-1918 boom, by the Attlee Government's decision to continue rationing and controls. With the end of the boom, GEC had a structure wholly unsuited to efficient operation. First, it pursued a declared policy of making all types of electrical goods; the company repeated on a large scale the classic industrial mistake of making things rather than money. Second, the strategy of the business was determined by production rather than sales. This was perhaps a natural result of the post-1939 era, when capacity was the limiting factor, first to meet the war effort and later to satisfy pent-up demand. But GEC's production orientation had serious drawbacks. First, products were made to standards of internal excellence, rather than aimed at a particular market. Second, this often resulted in GEC making the wrong things: among many stories was the warehouse full of surplus bedwarmers and the stockpile of lightning conductors at Magnet House. Third, GEC lacked an effective system of finance and cost control. It combined centralization of decisions with no effective power from the centre over its components: a structure not unlike the Turkish empire of the late nineteenth century, which produced rather similar results.

GEC Under Pressure

Two years passed, while GEC's trading and financial position steadily deteriorated. Lindley set in motion a rationalization of sales and a slimming down of the central headquarters. His strategy was broadly correct, but the pace was too slow and it was not certain whether he would have acted firmly towards the manufacturing units of GEC. In 1963, with GEC's problems becoming more acute and more obvious, two directors visited Weinstock to ask him to become managing director. The following four years, from 1963 to 1967, saw Weinstock transform GEC from a large, ailing company, into a slimmer, efficient, industrial group. Kenneth Bond, working closely with Weinstock, also played a key role in this transformation. This achievement made Weinstock a familiar name in the City and business; he became the archetype of the modern successful and, if necessary, ruthless chief executive. The shortest summary of Weinstock's achievements in those years lies in GEC's financial results:

	GEC sales (£m)	Before tax profits (£m)	Return on capital employed (%)
1968	198	21·3	19·2
1967	180	17·7	17·4
1966	169	19·5	19·8
1965	170	17·4	18·0
1964	158	11·8	13·0
1963	147	6·1	7·9
1962	135	4·1	6·5

It was during these years also that a mythology, a kind of superficial, accepted wisdom, grew up. Weinstock was considered to be a man whose skills lay in pruning, closing out of date factories, and making workers redundant. The sale of a large and prestigious central office became a symbol of his method of operation. (Magnet House, GEC-AEI's head-quarters, was sold during the bid. English Electric's head office in the Strand was also sold.) But these were simply the more obvious results of Weinstock's policy. His essential strategy, which was crucial to the reviving of GEC and later to the reshaping of AEI and the merger with English Electric, lay in three lines of approach. The first was to devolve full responsibility to operating executives; the head of an operating unit was transformed from a kind of super civil servant, a hierarchical figure responsible to head office, into an executive with full accountability. Second, Weinstock instituted a close and effective system of financial control which was sophisticated yet did not obstruct successful operations. Third, Weinstock enforced these criteria fairly, but firmly; if a senior executive failed to meet his financial standards and failed to master the business then he was sacked. By 1966–67, GEC had established a strong financial and trading position. Weinstock's system was well established, GEC had moved out of heavy electrical engineering, and its growing potential lay in electronics and telecommunications.

At AEI, GEC's large rival, these years saw an accumulation of problems fully as serious as those of the old GEC. AEI's financial record tells the story; under Lord Chandos' chairmanship, AEI had expanded too fast into general electrical engineering. Like the old GEC, AEI believed in making everything electrical It was divided into two powerful and selfwilled empires, British Thomson Houston at Rugby and Metrovick at Manchester. Again, like the old GEC, AEI lacked any system of financial control, combining a substantial degree of centralization with little effective power over the operating units. Sir Charles Wheeler succeeded Lord Chandos as chairman, but executive control lay with Sir Joseph Latham who embarked on reorganization and imported outside executives, such as John Barber from Ford as finance director and Nigel Maclean as commercial director. By

1967, Latham's reorganization had not visibly proceeded beyond diagnosis towards discernible action. Barber set up an elaborate system for collecting financial information. While Sir Joseph Latham's plans represented a great advance for AEI, it is not clear whether he and his team would have successfully solved the critical problems, such as the BTH-Metrovick rivalry.

Telephone Rentals Setback

About this time, the end of 1966, Weinstock launched a large (£24 million) but ultimately unsuccessful bid for Telephone Rentals. The contest was based on finely drawn terms. The board benefited from good advice but some tactical opportunities were missed. But the Telephone Rentals affair was soon to be forgotten in the battle for AEI. (Telephone Rentals apart, Weinstock made only two substantial acquisitions during his years at GEC: Cannon Holdings in 1964 and, in 1966, a share interest in Woods, the Xpelair company; at Radio and Allied, he had taken over McMichael for £345 000.)

The slow recovery at AEI might have shown successes if allowed time and reasonable trading conditions, but the entire electrical industry scenario was to be transformed by a *deus ex machina* from Whitehall.

The structure of Britain's electrical industry was transformed as a result of action intended to avert the serious results of a collapse in orders from the Central Electricity Generating Board. One of the most serious industrial problems facing the Labour Government which came to power in 1964 was the threat of a run down in power station orders. Slow economic growth and growing competition from oil threatened to turn a serious situation into one of near crisis. A brief for action was prepared in the newly created Department of Economic Affairs, and the Industrial Reorganization Corporation, set up in 1966, was given the job of solving the problems of Britain's heavy electrical industry as a high priority.

In the early 'sixties the CEGB had embarked on an ambitious programme of power station construction. It was reacting to the power shortages of the 'fifties, and based its forecasts on maintained rapid growth in the industrial demand for electricity. Above all, the power station programme was based on the 3·8 per cent annual growth which was set out in the National Plan. All these forecasts proved overoptimistic: against the assumption of a 3·8 per cent growth rate, itself a marked advance on the British norm of 2·9 per cent, economic expansion averaged only a 2·3 per cent rate from 1964 to 1969. The CEGB also overestimated the pace at which the demand for electricity would grow compared with industrial production as a whole – mainly because oil proved an effective competitor. The full extent of this overoptimism did not appear immediately, because five to six years elapse between the approval of a power station and its commissioning. From 1961

16

to 1963, the CEGB launched a heavy approvals programme, involving nearly 16 500 MW, programmed for 1966 to 1968. Even as late as 1965, the CEGB forecast a maximum demand of 54 000 MW for the winter of 1970–71; this was, in the event, exactly the same forecast total as the CEGB projected in 1970 for the winter of 1975–76. The CEGB had compressed sufficient orders for virtually the whole decade into the first five years.

By 1965–66, with the extent of the CEGB's overoptimism beginning to become apparent, its previous massive approvals programme was equally massively cut back. Compared with the 16 500 MW of 1961 to 1963, the CEGB approved 7700 MW in the three years 1965 to 1967 for completion in 1970 to 1972. This cutback affected ancillary equipment, such as transformers and switchgear, even harder than heavy engineering. New orders for transformers by the electricity authorities fell from an average of £42·5 million a year from 1964 to 1967 to £7·7 million in 1968; orders for switchgear from electricity and other industries dropped from £60 million to £70 million in 1963 to £20 million in 1968.

From 1966 onwards, these trends were fully appreciated in Whitehall. Such a severe and sudden contraction would affect the big three electrical groups: English Electric, AEI, and Reyrolle-Parsons, to whom GEC had sold their heavy electrical interests. It was feared that none of the three would make profits, that design teams might be dispersed, and future growth prospects damaged. Whitehall's plan was to bring about rationalization; to reduce the three major units to two. AEI stood out as the weakest in financial and managerial terms. GEC had established its managerial skills and had moved out of heavy electrical engineering. What was more natural, therefore, than that GEC should take over AEI and reorganize its heavy electrical interests in association with English Electric and Reyrolle-Parsons? This seemed good sense to everyone, with the conspicuous and important exception of AEI itself.

IRC's Plan

The IRC, whose chief executive was Ronald Grierson, the former merchant banker, was entrusted with the rationalization of the electrical industry. Grierson asked Hill Samuel, the City bank to draw up plans for a merger between GEC and AEI; Grierson established that GEC would be willing to take over AEI, with consent from the IRC. GEC considered that government backing would be helpful after, rather than during, the merger. The GEC board seem to have been influenced partly by prospects of the damage likely to be inflicted on the entire industry by the CEGB's prospective cutback and partly by the attraction of putting right, in ways which had already proved successful, the manifold problems of AEI. AEI soon made it clear that it did not want a merger with GEC; but GEC's enthusiasm was growing and Sir Frank, later Lord, Kearton, the chairman of the IRC, was pressing for vigorous action. The upshot was that on 28 September 1967 GEC put a takeover offer to AEI, to launch what proved to be a three-month, bitter, but ultimately successful, takeover fight.

GEC began by offering some £120 million for AEI, or about 25 per cent above the prevailing stock market price. The heart of AEI's defence, published three weeks after GEC's approach, lay in its forecast of sharply improved profits: £10 million for 1967 against £9·2 million the previous year, rising to £16 million for 1968, and £20 million for 1969. The AEI board also produced a new chairman elect, in the person of Lord Beeching, formerly of ICI and well known for his rationalization of the railways. AEI also launched more controversial moves, notably the sale of the minority interest in British Lighting Industries to Thorn Electrical for £12·3 million. AEI also proposed to merge its telecommunications business with that of the US owned Standard Telephones and Cables, but this latter transaction was made dependent on defeat of the GEC bid. Sir Joseph Latham, in his subsequent book on the bid, *Takeover*, defended the sale of British Lighting shares as being consistent with previous boardroom strategy. But the transaction attracted severe criticism, for it appeared that the disposal of an important asset during the course of a takeover bid could become an attempt to frustrate the bid itself. AEI also sold its head office to Land Securities, on terms which Land Securities was able to improve upon within a year.

At the same time, AEI sought to attract IRC support for its own rationalization. But Kearton, who was now handling the IRC side of the affair, made clear his view that AEI's rationalization was too little and too late. He also hinted at reservations about the proposed deal with Standard Telephones. AEI's forecasts presented a new situation for GEC, who at the end of October raised its bid by £32 million to £152 million which AEI rejected. Only a few days later, GEC raised its bid for a second time by a further £8 million to £160 million, which again brought rejection from AEI. GEC also attacked AEI's profit forecasts which it argued should be treated 'with considerable caution'. Each side was making efforts to put its case to the major shareholders. In a series of meetings up and down the country, Lord Aldington and Arnold Weinstock spoke for GEC, while Sir Joseph Latham and John Barber argued for AEI. GEC's final offer closed in early November; by the late evening of 8 November, GEC had some 44 per cent acceptances for its offer – a close but decisive result. Looking back now, it is surprising that AEI was able to limit the initial response to GEC's bid. There seem to be three major reasons why GEC secured a satisfactory, rather than immediately overwhelming, victory. One, paradoxically, was the support of the IRC, though Lord Kearton played a subsidiary role during the takeover battle. Many fund managers and others in the City resented intervention by a Labour Government in industry, and decided, therefore, to withhold support from GEC. The second factor was AEI's established

18

position and powerful connections in industry and the City. AEI's board included influential outside directors, and the company's standing weighed against its poor financial record. The initial 44 per cent acceptances received by GEC included relatively few from City and investment institutions. Arnold Weinstock was assured of victory by the broad mass of public shareholders in AEI. The Prudential Assurance, for once, did not give the City institutions a lead; normally a powerful champion of shareholders' rights, the Prudential was in a particularly difficult situation. Some time before, it had made discreet approaches to AEI about the management and financial situation to which the AEI board had reacted favourably. For this reason, the Prudential felt itself committed to supporting the AEI board. The Pru's apparent coolness towards the GEC bid, for reasons not fully appreciated, may have influenced a number of City institutions. The Church Commissioners, by contrast, accepted the GEC bid. The third reason why GEC's bid did not do better in the City was a sharp burst of antisemitic feeling. For some, Weinstock was in error not merely for being Jewish, but for showing a particularly British concern just how badly it was being run.

Forecast Confounded

There were two sequels to GEC's conquest of AEI. One was the confounding of the 1967 profit forecast, when in mid 1968 GEC revealed that AEI had made a loss of £4·5 million against the £10 million projected profit. Two distinguished firms of auditors put down this £14·5 million difference to £5 million of fact and £9·5 of judgement. The second sequel was Sir Joseph Latham's expression of his version of the bid in his book *Takeover*. As a detailed narrative of AEI's recent history, Latham's book was less than complete; he defended the AEI directors and argued that AEI had been taken over because of its profit record. But before Latham's book appeared and before the AEI victory was barely a year old, Arnold Weinstock had completed his dominance of British electrical engineering by merging with English Electric.

Immediately after the takeover of AEI, Weinstock began talks with Lord Nelson, chairman of English Electric, on the rationalization of the two groups' heavy electrical interests: this was, after all, the problem which had originally sparked off the merger. What precipitated the GEC-English Electric alliance was an attempt by Plessey, whose assets were barely one-third of English Electric's, to take over the larger company. Plessey employed its capital more profitably, but the sight of a company making £16 million a year trying to take over an unwilling partner making £20 million a year startled both the industry and Whitehall. For the Clark brothers, who ran Plessey, GEC's acquisition of AEI had produced a change in the balance of power, not unlike Chrysler's buying into Rootes which precipitated the reshaping of the British motor industry. Plessey's original hope seems to have been that it might take over International Computers (created out of Powers-Samas and International Tabulating), which carried the government's undertaking to maintain a British computer industry.

Plessey's hopes of taking over ICL were finally frustrated by a massive compromise, which gave just over half the equity to former shareholders in International Computers and Tabulators, and left Plessey, English Electric (which put its System 4 interests into the new company), and the government as minority shareholders. The Clark brothers had seized the idea that the electrical engineering business was both big and international. A subsequent Plessey statement said: 'To compete effectively calls for resources in the same range as those of the international giants.' When the attempted takeover of English Electric failed, Plessey moved into an alliance with a US group, Alloys Unlimited, whose acquisition both enlarged Plessey's size and gave it an international spread.

Weinstock Welcomed

As Lord Nelson had already been talking to Weinstock, the Plessey offer, which Nelson was advised he might not be able to resist on financial grounds, had the effect of bringing English Electric and GEC together. This may have surprised Plessey, but Weinstock had impressed the industry with the care with which he had explained his aims in taking over AEI. Lord Nelson himself was aware of government pressures, while a number of English Electric's senior managers approved of Weinstock's methods.

Plessey and its advisers, Warburgs, then made a change of front. Instead of seeking to contest the bid, Warburgs themselves issued a rather enigmatic statement urging talks to rationalize the electrical engineering industry. British Insulated Callenders Cables as well as Plessey was concerned at the consequences of GEC, which had already absorbed AEI, also taking over English Electric. Their fundamental cause for concern lay in the prospective change in the balance of power. They and others were concerned that a major group, with annual sales and assets of about £1000 million, would be able to exercise a dominant influence. There also seems to have been a fear that a large diversified giant like GEC-English Electric could use its overall financial resources to undercut its competitors in particular sectors. Lord Nelson himself suggested that Hawker Siddeley or Reyrolle-Parsons might feel threatened by the merger.

In the event, the consortium to oppose the merger never got off the ground, though Lord Mcfadzean, chairman of BICC, resigned from the English Electric board when a merger with GEC-AEI seemed likely. The problem facing this consortium, like so many others, was that its members were united primarily over a negative objective, to stop a particular bid. The prime movers, Plessey and BICC, realized that international development represented the most sensible alternative and each of them formed an association with a

20

major US group, Plessey with Alloys Unlimited and BICC with General Cables. The merger between English Electric and GEC-AEI went ahead, greatly helped by Lord Aldington, chairman of GEC-AEI, offering to step down to the deputy chairmanship in order to give the chair to Lord Nelson.

It will take at least five years to pass a final verdict on the merger between GEC, AEI, and English Electric. But the first stages of Weinstock's integration are worth setting out as a guide to the future, as well as illustrating his overall plan of campaign.

This plan, which took some time to unfold, carried the blessing of the IRC and (after some debate) that of the Labour Cabinet through the Board of Trade. The IRC, which listened to both GEC's and Plessey's cases for taking over English Electric, as well as those of their principal customers, argued that the GEC-English Electric merger '. . . is a further major step in promoting the efficiency, profitability and potential of the electrical and electronics industry . . .' The government, therefore, because of the 'damaging effect of uncertainty and delay' did not refer the merger to the Monopolies Commission: the Commission, therefore, did not investigate three of the largest among recent mergers, namely GEC's two takeovers and BMC-Leyland. GEC-English Electric gave Whitehall assurances over regional and redundancy policy, which have become features of all large mergers, and undertook to 'avoid policies directed towards damaging fair and effective competition'. There was also a proposal to appoint an IRC director to the GEC board, but this was not pursued.

During the first two years of the merger, Weinstock reduced the three companies' combined labour force by between 15000 and 20000, or close to 10 per cent of the total. Contrary to widespread belief, Weinstock did not base his methods on large scale labour redundancies. At GEC, he held the labour force at a fixed level, while raising the ratio of sales and profits per employee. Many of the redundancies came from reorganization, which the two and later three electrical giants clearly needed. In the spring of 1969, Weinstock assured Labour backbenchers that social demands affected management planning—though he complained how difficult it proved to carry through agreements made with national union leaders at the local level. The apparent slimming down of the labour force was also exaggerated by the disposal of companies. This is reflected in the decline, by 23000, of the home labour force of the three companies between the autumn of 1968 and the spring of 1970. Most of the redundancies were concentrated on the heavy electrical side, where substantial surplus capacity existed. Foreseeably, Weinstock disposed of English Electric's valuable head office in London, releasing both assets and executive staff.

Woolwich Closure

Many of the work-force reductions were concentrated in three major moves: the closing of AEI's former telecommunications factory at Woolwich early in 1968; the reorganization of the transformer side in the summer of the following year; and an allied reshuffle of power engineering in the autumn of 1969. The closing of Woolwich was the first major closure carried out after the AEI takeover. As a result, it received considerable publicity and it proved a model of how to close a factory. Woolwich was the former Siemens factory. Over one hundred years old, it formed part of AEI Telecommunications which had lost more than £3 million in 1966–67. Some 6000 extra staff had been recruited by AEI Telecommunications in the previous two years, though AEI Telecommunications produced only half as much as GEC Telecommunications from a larger factory area. Its work force was about 80 per cent of GEC, but generating sales only 60 per cent as large. At Woolwich, AEI developed System 18, a private venture telephone exchange for which no orders had appeared. The factory concentrated on Strowger telephone exchanges, which the Post Office was gradually phasing out and which were also made more efficiently by AEI in Scotland and the North East and by GEC at Coventry. Woolwich was a big factory employing 5500 in a busy part of South East London. Strong competition in telecommunications and the ending of bulk supply agreements by the Post Office meant that action could not be delayed.

The original proposal to close Woolwich, which seems to have originated with George Tomlin, head of GEC Telecommunications at Coventry, followed the closing of a factory at Sydenham which employed just over 500 people making private telephone systems. The decision to close Woolwich, which was made public on 1 February 1968, brought a storm of protest from the workers, trade unions, local MP's, and councillors. The closing of Woolwich Arsenal some years before had only just been absorbed. GEC offered Woolwich staff jobs in its other Strowger plants, but these were accepted by relatively few workers. The greater part of the Woolwich operation, therefore, centred on GEC's ability to ease redundancy. This was achieved in three ways: by offering redundancy payments 50 per cent higher than the government scheme; through special payments, two-thirds salary for six months, for men out of work for more than one month; and by offering a loyalty bonus to production staff who stayed at Woolwich in order to keep the factory going. The Department of Employment and Productivity organized help by arranging links with nearby labour exchanges, visits to alternative employers, and so on. From a social point of view, the closing of Woolwich worked much better than had been originally forecast. Peter Shore, as Minister for Economic Affairs, explained how after ten months 4600 out of 5000 had found alternative jobs. From GEC's standpoint, the closure demonstrated that the new group was prepared to take decisive and unpopular action. But Woolwich was an expensive operation, precisely how expensive has never been clear. Probably more important, it proved a major distraction for management time; and the effects of the publicity which inevitably surrounded the first big closure may have slowed down the reorganization of telecommunications.

BTH-Metrovick

Weinstock's reshaping of the heavy electrical side, where the strategy became apparent in the summer of 1969, was of fundamental importance for the development of the combined group. By then he had achieved the decisive management feat, which had perpetually eluded AEI, of making British Thomson Houston and Metrovick work together. Weinstock also exploded the belief that GEC was the privileged member of the merger, by closing GEC's transformer division at Witton. This was a smaller operation than Woolwich, though it meant some 2500 workers looking for jobs outside the merger group.

The third major area of redundancy strategy, the slimming down of power engineering during the autumn of 1969, involving about 3500 men mainly on Merseyside, was perhaps the least surprising of all. A key role in this was played by Sir Jack Scamp, a director of GEC since 1962, who had become the country's leading investigator and conciliator of industrial disputes. GEC set out the logic of its plans in a characteristically detailed assessment to national union officials in July that year. Power engineering production, it was explained, was carried on in forty-three separate locations with a total work force of 54000. In the face of the drop in orders from the CEGB, a low rate 'expected to continue for some years', GEC and AEI showed 'extensive duplication of products and facilities'. On turbine generators, employing just under 12000, the decline in CEGB ordering was accompanied by a sharp rise in the size of individual sets; in other words, smaller business was spread over fewer units, creating a 'serious excess' of capacity. The package involved a reduction in the work force of about 3850, or 7 per cent of the group total, between mid 1969 and the end of 1970. Typical was the reasoning behind the decision not to place power engineering work at Netherton: 'There is no prospect whatsoever of a successful and stable business being re-created and sustained in water turbines and special pumps...' Analysing English Electric's loss-making water turbine division, GEC pointed out that European and Japanese manufacturers offered prices 20 to 40 per cent below the estimated total cost of British manufacture, which itself showed a 'total inability to meet the estimated erection costs'.

Management Methods

The results of Weinstock's work at GEC are now well known; his work at AEI is beginning to emerge; and the full results of the GEC-AEI-EE merger will inevitably take some time to appear. What is equally important is how Weinstock manages: a successful basis for running large diversified companies should be of great value to British industrial development. The

23

notion that his skill lies primarily in pruning is a myth; equally untrue, and favoured by some of Weinstock's critics, is the belief that he gets results at the expense of long term profits, say by cutting back on research. In reality, group spending on research and development runs at £60 million a year and the principal evidence of the new regime's belief in research was the appointment of a technical director in addition to a director of research. In the pre-merger GEC, no less than 20 per cent of output in 1966 derived from research and development which had come to fruition in the two previous years.

How does Weinstock manage? The short answer is that he gives the heads of manufacturing divisions great, almost entrepreneurial, freedom. At every point in the chain of command, there is an identifiable individual who can be held responsible. These individuals are not directed managerially from the centre nor are they asked to support a large headquarters operation. But this entrepreneurial freedom is subject to simple, carefully defined, financial criteria which lie at the heart of Weinstock's management system. If the independent manufacturing heads persistently fail to meet these criteria without good cause, then, in the last resort, they are sacked. Being sacked is, after all, the corollary of being left free; the use of financial criteria means that dismissal stems from poor performance, not from any lack of social background or political skills. The monthly financial reports are closely scrutinized by an informal but highly effective system: there is little formal structure at the top of GEC; Weinstock himself rarely attends meetings.

It is easy to see how AEI, and many large British companies, fail by these standards. Divisional heads are rarely dismissed nor are they left free – hence they have few inducements to show good performance. They are subject to elaborate, rather than simple, financial controls behind which lies no effective deterrent. Even an enterprising manager will be pushed into the position where his prime aim will be to avoid making a mistake.

Weinstock's methodology thus rests crucially on his financial standards, on which, as the quotation at the beginning of the chapter explains, he spends much time. Weinstock's seven standards were set out in my article which appeared in *The Times Business News* of November 1968. Weinstock uses seven ratios, three for profits and four for sales: profits on capital employed, on sales, and per employee; and sales as a ratio of capital employed, fixed assets, stocks, and per employee. These ratios were built up partly out of Weinstock's own experience and partly from comparison with successful US electrical groups such as General Electric and Texas Instruments. For a manufacturing unit, the ability of capital to generate profits is the most fundamental of the seven. But generalization is difficult: only if all seven indicators are showing favourably can it be certain that the company is performing well. A comparison of US with British companies throws up fascinating results. While profit margins are

24

roughly similar, British companies use on average about twice as much capital to generate a given volume of sales. The ratio of stocks to total sales is lower in the US, probably reflecting the more effective use of computer and control techniques allied to greater technical skills at lower and middle management level. Another contributory factor is the better service received by large US companies from their components and materials suppliers.

Any man who rescued one major company and then took over two others between his mid thirties and mid forties would deserve a place in business history, though Weinstock is very different from some other executive heads of large companies. His public appearances are rare, and he avoids making political and social comment, though he holds characteristically well defined views. Public recognition came in the summer of 1970, when he was knighted 'For services to export'. Sir Arnold Weinstock emerges as the one major industrialist since the Second World War to have devised, and put to successful effect, new methods of industrial operation. For this reason in addition even to its sheer size, GEC-AEI-EE could prove the most important among recent industrial mergers.

BMC and Leyland = British Leyland

The creation of British Leyland Motor Corporation in early 1968, through the alliance of Leyland with British Motor Holdings, ranks as the largest industrial merger in Britain's history. British Leyland then employed nearly 200 000 people throughout the world and had total sales of about £800 million a year. It ranked second only to Volkswagen as the largest motor manufacturer outside the US. In Britain, it rated as the fifth largest company, and ranked second to ICI as the largest British manufacturer. British Leyland had nearly 250 000 shareholders holding an equity valued at nearly £450 million, backed by assets of more than £300 million.

British Motor Corporation itself, which in effect was taken over by Leyland, had been created in 1952 by the major industrial merger in early postwar Britain. BMC represented the uniting of Austin and Morris, two of the best known names in the motor vehicle industry. A merger between the two had been discussed before the Second World War, but this only became a reality post 1945, after the death of Austin and with the imminent retirement of William Morris, Lord Nuffield. In the late 'forties, a merger was actively discussed, but it was decided that the time was not right. Instead, the two companies agreed to standardize certain functional components which would not affect their individuality. According to Philip Andrews, the official biographer of Lord Nuffield, this agreement was 'not immediately effective' because of prevailing competition between Austin and Morris. But with Nuffield's decision to retire, merger talks proceeded and, in 1952, the creation of BMC was finally agreed. Nuffield had himself decided to hand over to Sir Leonard Lord, who had started in the drawing-office at Hotchkiss, later to become Morris Engines (Coventry). An apprentice in that same drawing-office was a young man called George Harriman, whose father had worked in the business and whose close association with Lord was to dominate BMC throughout a generation; the same George Harriman became the first president of British Leyland.

Lord took the chair at BMC six months after the merger, with Nuffield as honorary president. Lord, an autocratic and remote figure, remained in control of BMC for the next nine years. He was succeeded by Harriman in 1961, after the latter had become managing director five years earlier.

26

Lord set the seal on the future of BMC; the major criticism of Lord, later Lord Lambury, was that he perpetuated the major differences between Austin and Morris. Lord himself had had an unusual career; having re-organized Wolseley for William Morris, he resigned in 1936 to become managing director of Austin. Both he and Harriman were Austin men, and it was said that there was a steady 'Austin influence', that integration was not pursued because a policy of 'creative tensions' was fostered by Lord. In fairness, his position as an ex-Austin man was far from easy. Morris shareholders had gained the major slice of BMC's capital (£2·65 million out of a total £4·83 million), while Nuffield continued to maintain an office in BMC and took lunch with his colleagues daily for several years after the merger had gone through. Moreover, the Nuffield Foundation remained the largest single shareholder in BMC. It enjoys the same position in British Leyland, controlling just over 10 per cent of the ordinary capital.

When Lord became chairman of BMC, the shortage of new cars in Britain was just coming to an end. The years of his chairmanship still saw the production, rather than the selling, of cars as the industry's main problem. With hindsight, it is clear that during these years BMC failed to realize the potential benefits of integration and large scale production; at the same time, it invested too little in new capital. BMC began with 40 per cent of the British car market, but saw its share slowly eroded over the years almost wholly to the benefit of Ford – while independents like Jowett, Singer, Alvis, and eventually Standard, all disappeared. In the years 1952 to 1956 BMC, although larger than Ford, ploughed back only some £45 million against the US controlled company's £60 million. As Silberston and Maxcy, writing in the late 'fifties, have pointed out, while BMC was the biggest British vehicle manufacturer, making some 440000 vehicles in the year to July 1956, it is doubtful whether any one model was produced on a scale of much over 100000 a year. During the decade 1956 to 1965, BMC's market share fluctuated between 43 per cent and 39 per cent (it dipped to 35 per cent in 1953). During the same years, Ford's share virtually doubled from just over 14 per cent to 27 per cent.

Production Battle

BMC's strong market position during the postwar years rested on the Morris Minor launched in 1948, followed by the A30 three years later. To match these, Ford had one basic small model, the Anglia. But, as Silberston and Maxcy again point out, in the crucial battle for production, Ford moved ahead of BMC: during the first fifteen postwar years, Ford's output went up by 60 per cent against a rise of 20 per cent by BMC.

At this time, Leyland was building its extremely successful export record. At the time of the BMC merger, Leyland counted for less than 5 per cent of commercial vehicle sales in Britain with an annual production of 10000 units. But in the category of heavy vehicles, buses, road tankers, and so on, Leyland and Associated Commercial Vehicles together, out of a total of twenty manufacturers, supplied more than 50 per cent of all vehicles. During the first postwar decade, Britain's exports of commercial vehicles far outpaced that of any of her major competitors; exports grew roughly four-fold from some 45000 in 1946 to just over 150000 in 1955. During these same years, US exports remained roughly static at about 175000; German exports, which were virtually nil in the early postwar years, had reached about 70000 by the mid 'fifties.

A major decision made by Lord during this period was to buy the body supplier Fisher and Ludlow, then a £4·5 million company. This was largely a defensive measure, which followed the acquisition of Briggs Motor Bodies by Ford. BMC's move was an intriguing pointer to the acquisition of Pressed Steel in 1965; Fisher and Ludlow also made bodies for Standard, then a thriving independent, who moved its custom to Pressed Steel (rather than see its body supplies come under the control of a competitor) and later bought Mulliner as a body supplier.

The year 1961, when Harriman took over as chairman of BMC, was a turning-point both for his company and for the British motor industry. Two years before, BMC had launched the Mini, an adventurous but rather crudely finished car which was just beginning to prove a success. Sir Alec Issigonis, its designer, later explained: 'The Mini was a car born of necessity . . . there was petrol rationing and the Suez crisis and my own personal hunch that there was a need for a compact car with four seats.'

Rootes' Problems

But what made 1961 so important for the British industry and, in the event, for BMC itself, were far reaching moves at Rootes and Ford. Rootes provided one of the major talking points for British industry during 1961, when Lord Rootes, William Rootes, its founder, decided to fight out a bitter industrial dispute at the company's Acton plant. This dispute, the British Light Steel Pressings strike, was a victory for Rootes, but achieved at great cost to the company. In the previous year, the Rootes board had decided to launch a new small car, the Hillman Imp. This was intended to be a sophisticated and rather more expensive version of the Mini, built with a rear, aluminium engine. The strategy behind the decision was sound, but there were two grave faults in Rootes' planning. First, it was too late. Rootes' directors reached their decision a year after the Mini had appeared: the Imp was ready for sale in 1963, four years after the Mini, which had by then established a commanding market position. The other strategic defect in the plan, which was forced on Rootes by Whitehall, was the location of the Imp's production. Rootes later explained that a site was available on land adjoining the Dunstable factory but the company was 'persuaded' by the government to establish an entirely new plant at Linwood in Renfrewshire, as part of the official programme to stimulate economic development in Scotland. This was part of the policy which sent BMC to Bathgate, and Ford, Vauxhall, and Triumph to North West England. Whatever may have been the social and political advantages of this policy, and these seem not to have been carefully evaluated, the direct costs were great. Rootes had to employ a labour force with little skill in relatively sophisticated engineering, and which enjoyed a bad record of labour disputes. Productivity at Linwood compared badly with that at Rootes factories in the Midlands; at one stage, the aluminium engines for the Imp had to be shipped back to Coventry for completion before being returned to Scotland. In 1965, Rootes gave a cool but revealing résumé of its experience at Linwood:

> We anticipated that a major expansion . . . would present us with a number of problems. In the event the difficulties turned out to be even greater than we had foreseen and the Linwood project has proved to be a great financial drain . . .

By the mid 'sixties, thanks to the Acton strike and the launching of the Imp, Rootes was financially vulnerable. But a takeover was bound to produce a drastic change in the balance of power in the British motor industry. The fact that the takeover eventually came from a US group, Chrysler, provoked a reshaping of the entire industry.

The other major development of 1961 was the decision, taken by Ford of Detroit, to buy out the minority shareholders in Ford of Dagenham. By the standards of those days, this was a massive takeover, which involved the transfer of some £130 million cash from US Ford to British shareholders and provided a useful benefit for Britain's gold reserves. The terms of the takeover were hotly disputed, and one of British Ford's large institutional shareholders stood out against the bid. From the trade unions, there was concern that Ford's move might point to a shift in resources away from Dagenham towards Cologne – a move which ironically was given credibility by Ford's difficult labour relations and the problems of handling twenty or so unions at their British factories.

US Ford's Strategy

What received less attention at the time was the strategy which lay behind US Ford's bid. This was two-fold. One aim was to internationalize the overseas operations of US Ford. Detroit aimed to operate both German and British Ford (French Ford had been disposed of some years before) as part of a global strategy. The full implications of Ford's plans only became clear years later, with the simultaneous launch of a major model, the Capri, in Britain and Germany. But the essential point was that Ford, like General Motors, had realized much earlier than the European companies that the motor car market was becoming international, and that the transnational planning of production and marketing was now essential. The second element in Ford's strategy was to be able to develop Ford of Dagenham without being concerned specifically with short term profits and dividends. Ford planned to carry out a massive investment programme in Britain and Germany, even at the expense of short term profits, with a view to building up its medium and long term market position. Such a plan would have raised great problems for a medium sized, nationally based group such as BMC, even if the full extent of Ford's plans had been realized.

In these years, a major shift was taking place in the direction of government economic policy. Stop-go was developed in the 'sixties – an unpopular and ultimately unsuccessful policy which consisted of making abrupt short term changes, notably in hire purchase finance regulations and purchase tax, in order to sustain a positive balance of payments. Stop-go was supplemented only in the late 'sixties by a more sophisticated monetary policy, after both successive governments and the Treasury had realized the severe damage that was being inflicted on consumer-orientated industries. From 1964 onwards, stop-go did serious harm to the British motor industry and above all to the nationally based companies, such as BMC and Rootes, which did not command the financial resources of the US based transnationals. Selwyn Lloyd's restraints of 1961 brought car production down from 1·35 million to just over 1 million with sharp effects on BMC's profits. It was beginning to become clear that BMC had enjoyed a rather high break-even point over the years, the result of low capital investment, loose cost control, and unrealistic ideas of capacity. But in 1962, production revived to 1·25 million, rose again in 1963, and reached 1·87 million in 1964 – a level which was to prevail as a record. The period from 1962 to 1964 represents the golden years for the British motor industry.

It was also in 1961 that Leyland emerged once more as a car producer. Leyland returned to motor car production, a venture which in the 'twenties had brought the company near to bankruptcy, through the takeover of Standard. After the end of the sellers' market, car producers experienced serious difficulties: Jowett disappeared, Singer went to Rootes, Alvis to Rover, Daimler to Jaguar, and diversified groups like Hawker Siddeley quietly withdrew from car production. Standard, under the control of Alick Dick, who became chief executive while still under forty, was ill equipped to face the difficult conditions of the 'sixties. As a result, 1961 saw an agreed takeover by Leyland. The trio who had master-minded Leyland's striking progress since the Second World War, Sir Henry Spurrier, Donald Stokes, and Stanley Markland, moved into a company facing grave problems. Their first task was to bring about probably the most thorough-going reshuffle of top management ever after any merger in Britain. The majority of the Standard board was sacked. The Standard operation was reorganized by Stanley Markland. Under Donald Stokes' overall care (he succeeded Sir Henry Spurrier as chairman of Leyland in 1963) Standard production, sales, and servicing were reshaped. Even in the late 'sixties, it remained a profitable specialist car producer through a skilful policy of complementing, not competing with, BMC and Ford models.

During these years, Rootes' situation was growing more difficult. The cost of launching the Imp and its disappointing reception, together with the cost of the Acton strike, made its independent position untenable. Lord Rootes and his brother, Sir Reginald Rootes, began discussions with Chrysler. In retrospect, the choice of a US ally may seem unusual, but Chrysler, who had been making a rapid come-back as the third of the US automobile giants, lacked representation outside the US. While Chrysler controlled Simca in France and had an interest in Barreiros in Spain, it was anxious to move into Britain. An alliance with Rootes would clearly be far cheaper and quicker than starting car production from a green field. From Rootes' standpoint, only a major automobile group could offer the financial and technical expertise which it needed; and an alliance with either BMC or with Leyland would have meant that the family moved into second place. This was something which Rootes was concerned to avoid; the first stage of the Chrysler link-up preserved its independence while offering substantial help. In 1964, details were published of an alliance whereby Chrysler bought 40 per cent of the votes in Rootes and 50 per cent of the voteless capital. The alliance brought some misgivings from the Labour Opposition, notably Mr Wilson and Mr Callaghan; the Chancellor, Reginald Maudling, secured undertakings from Chrysler, notably that it would not seek to gain control of Rootes without prior consultation with the Treasury.

Pressed Steel's Position

Labour MPs' concern about the Chrysler-Rootes alliance was great enough; but it was fully matched by the profound reaction which the deal produced among the leaders of the British motor industry. The emergence in Britain of another major US car manufacturer posed questions enough. What precipitated the ensuing reshuffle of the motor industry, however, was the position of Pressed Steel, the major, independent producer of car bodies. Pressed Steel supplied all Rootes car bodies as well as sending bodies to BMC and to specialist producers such as Jaguar and Rover. At Linwood, Pressed Steel operated a large new plant specifically to supply bodies for the Imp. With Rootes now allied to a US giant, there was the clear prospect that Rootes would wish to control its own body supplies. But if Rootes, helped by Chrysler finance, made a bid for Pressed Steel, BMC and the specialists would be placed in a difficult position. BMC could, ironically, have faced the same position into which it had forced Standard a decade before by buying Fisher and Ludlow. So began the first round of merger talks in the industry, in this case between BMC, Pressed Steel – built up by Joe Edwards, lately of BMC, into a highly efficient organization – and Jaguar.

The new Labour Government, elected in the autumn of 1964, was informed of these plans and explained that there would be no official objections; already fears of US industrial domination were beginning to bother Labour Ministers. This first round of merger talks, which lasted for several months, finally broke down. Sir William Lyons, the highly successful head of Jaguar, wished to preserve his independence, and it was not yet clear that Chrysler, a large, but still a minority shareholder, in Rootes, would be able to move. But Sir George Harriman and Joe Edwards carried on discussions, which were underlined by the prospect that Edwards might help with the long needed management reshuffle at BMC. By the summer of the following year, negotiations were complete and BMC made an agreed takeover of Pressed Steel. This deal placed Rootes in a difficult position, for it now depended, at Linwood, on the supply of bodies from a major rival. Harriman explained that he had no wish to exploit this situation, and at the end of 1965 BMC agreed to sell the Linwood plant to Rootes; the bulk of the £14 million purchase price being represented by Board of Trade loans.

This deal gave the City and the motor industry an insight into Rootes' growing financial difficulties. If the British economy and the domestic sales of cars had expanded under the Wilson Government as they had from 1962 to 1964, there might have been a chance that Rootes could have retained some form of independence. But the early years of the Wilson Government, from 1964 onwards, saw a tight fiscal squeeze on the economy in order to sustain the balance of payments. The government had inherited a deficit, and compounded its economic problems by a series of gratuitous policy errors.

In the motor industry, production fell from 1·87 million vehicles in 1964 to 1·72 million in 1965, to 1·6 million in 1966, and to 1·55 million in 1967. These years of intensified stop-go pushed Rootes into the arms of Chrysler; they raised problems for even the strong specialist firms, and finally compelled BMC to merge with Leyland. Sir William Lyons, head of Jaguar, saw the direction which events were taking, and decided after all to merge with BMC. This deal, completed in the summer of 1966, reflected Sir George Harriman's concern not to let Jaguar fall to one of the rival groups. As the price for his consent, Sir William Lyons was able to exact an unusual degree of autonomy. 'Jaguar Cars will continue to operate as a separate entity and with the greatest practical degree of autonomy, under the chairmanship of Sir William Lyons', stated the formal merger document. The granting of such autonomy was very much in the old BMC tradition. Even if BMC, or British Motor Holdings as it was known after the Jaguar merger, had stayed independent, it was hard to see how integration could have been resisted for long.

The British Solution
Events now began to move rapidly. Only a few weeks after the merger

32

between BMC and Jaguar, Rootes and Chrysler called on Anthony Wedgwood-Benn, the Minister of Technology, whose department acted as sponsor for the motor industry. Rootes was in serious difficulties and needed a massive injection of new capital; Chrysler was prepared to step in, but in return it wanted voting and executive control of Rootes. This posed an acute problem for the Labour Cabinet; while in opposition, they had criticized the original Chrysler tie-up with Rootes in 1964, one of whose conditions was that Chrysler would not act to take control 'against the wishes of the British Government of the day'. Wedgwood-Benn called a series of meetings with Harriman and Stokes to see whether a 'British solution' for Rootes was possible. But Rootes' problems had grown too big: a short time later it was revealed that debts alone topped £40 million. Moreover, a British solution would probably have involved the closing of Linwood, which was politically impossible for a Labour Government. Rootes needed an immediate injection of £20 million of new capital, which Chrysler alone was in a position to supply. But before giving agreement, Wedgwood-Benn secured from Irving Minett, the Chrysler vice-president, a series of further conditions, notably that a majority of the Rootes directors should be British, and that there would be no impairment of development plans, particularly at Linwood.

Chrysler was then allowed to proceed with its takeover, but the affair had shaken the government's faith in Britain's ability to maintain an independent motor industry. From this point onwards, both the Prime Minister, Harold Wilson, and the Minister of Technology, Wedgwood-Benn, were convinced that a merger between BMC and Leyland was necessary. They pressed this view on Harriman, who was less enthusiastic, and on Stokes, whose appetite for the transaction grew over the months ahead. At that time, early 1967, all that appeared in public was a statement of the government's conviction 'that the British-controlled firms could gain greatly if they could co-operate much more fully in overseas marketing arrangements'. Wedgwood-Benn arranged for the IRC to discuss with BMC and Leyland closer co-ordination in their efforts overseas. The IRC, under Lord Kearton, had put money into Rootes. It was to play an important role in arranging the BMC-Leyland merger.

Labour Views

Why were Labour Ministers so keen on the merger? There were basically two reasons. One was that at that stage the Labour Cabinet was convinced of the great benefits of mergers to be achieved through economies in production, finance, and marketing; above all, Ministers were seized with the need for British companies to merge in order to be able to compete with their larger European and US counterparts. Professor Kaldor's thinking also influenced Labour Ministers; a key element of this was the economies effected by large scale production. Second, Harold Wilson and his Ministers began to take the view that the industrial future lay with professional, apolitical men who did not owe their position to social background or to accepted industrial traditions. As Ministers continued to press for a BMC-Leyland merger, criticism also began to mount of BMC's own shortcomings. To some degree, this criticism was justified, but BMC, a medium sized, national group, was suffering from the heavy capital spending programme launched by Ford after it won complete control of Dagenham in 1961, and from the successful return of General Motors' Vauxhall to the smaller car market.

BMC also suffered from the recession in the car industry which began in 1965. BMC, with its high break-even point, showed poor profits, and the setback in 1967 ended its hopes of independence – as it had ended those of Rootes. For all the problems at BMC, integration had not gone nearly far enough. BMC's commercial policy was criticized on the grounds that the group preferred to make cars rather than money. Its production control, too, was compared unfavourably with that of the US owned groups. Critics also pointed to the loose relationships between BMC and its distributors, who remained split between Austin and Morris. Probably the most disputed feature of BMC's production and sales policy was its 'badge engineering', the offering of different marques with broadly similar mechanical specifications. This was stoutly defended by Harriman, who argued that consumers were attached to names, as Indian buyers were to the Morris Oxford. Stokes made clear his dislike of badge engineering, and the general view was to contrast BMC's policy, unfavourably, with the GM-Ford way of offering different specifications, above all different engines, in the same marque's body. BMC cars, it was said, did not appear as a complete commercial package. The Mini, an outstanding engineering venture as an urban car, had poor ventilation and a mediocre gearbox. Given its generous dividend policy and high break-even point, BMC was caught in the familiar vicious circle of contraction because its cash flow was too small, which meant that it did not have sufficient profits to plough back for further development. The result was that by 1967–68, BMC's model range looked old: the Mini had been launched in 1959 and the 1100 five years later. BMC's big front-wheel drive car, the 1800, did not prove an immediate success, and its plans to launch an intermediate model, the 1500, ran into expensive and protracted difficulties; the car provided one of Stokes' earliest problems after the merger.

In early 1967, the initial reshaping of the British car industry was completed, when Rover joined Leyland. The move was a foreseeable one, after Jaguar had linked with BMC the previous year, but for Leyland the merger brought useful benefits. It greatly enlarged the group's base in the car industry, and offered immediate gains through economies in distribution in overseas markets such as Australia and South Africa. Serious merger talks between BMC and Leyland began in the autumn of 1967. The political

34

pressures were becoming hard to fight against. At a meeting with Stokes and Harriman, the Prime Minister put his view that the two companies should merge. Moreover, during these critical months, Harriman was often not entirely fit, and had to go into hospital for treatment of a stomach complaint. As 1967 wore on, it was becoming clear that the state of the car industry was pointing towards a merger. At the Longbridge headquarters of BMC (affectionately known as the Kremlin), there was no great enthusiasm for a merger, a view based partly on reaction to Leyland as newcomers to the car industry. There was also the view that BMC could solve its own, admitted, problems. This was based on the return of Joe Edwards, as chief executive of BMC, from the middle of 1966. Edwards was an old BMC man who had acquired an impressive reputation by his running of Pressed Steel. Edwards was widely admired as one of the best of the old school – tough, pragmatic, and immensely energetic. He now returned to BMC and began a carefully planned campaign to restore the group's fortunes. He imported men from Ford and laid plans to modernize BMC's ageing model range.

1967 Setback

But all these hopes at BMC were frustrated by the disastrous financial results for the year which ended in July 1967. Although the group had in- cluded Jaguar since the previous autumn, sales fell from £526 million to £467 million. For an organization like BMC with a high break-even point, this drop in sales hit profits badly, and the group showed a £3·4 million loss against the previous year's before tax profit of £20 million. BMC, for the first time in its fifteen-year history, cut its dividend from 20 per cent to 10 per cent. In the City, BMC's share price began to revive only because a bid from Leyland was considered, after these disappointing figures, to be inevitable. While Leyland's takeover of Aveling-Barford put its total market value just ahead of that of BMC.

The IRC began to play a key part in the talks. The turning-point in the negotiations was the question of management control. The original plan was that Harriman would be chairman, though it was conceded that he would delegate day to day executive responsibilities. Harriman first suggested that there should be two managing directors, Donald Stokes and Joe Edwards, each responsible to the chairman. But the Leyland board was adamant, and insisted that Stokes should be sole chief executive, with all executive directors reporting to him direct. He was quite prepared to welcome Joe Edwards as an executive director but not as his equal, and he was supported by the government, expressed through the Ministry of Technology and the IRC. Westminster had come to accept that, in managerial terms, the deal should be a takeover of BMC by Leyland and not a merger between the two.

The decisive meetings took place during the weekend before the final announcement on 16 January 1968. Harriman asked Edwards to come to

London for meetings on the Sunday, and left Edwards to dine at the Hyde Park Hotel with Lady Harriman while he went off to Donald Stokes' flat off St James's. After several hours of negotiations a tired Harriman returned about midnight with Kearton (chairman of IRC), and asked Edwards to join the meeting.

Harriman told Edwards that the deal had been agreed, but the two sides wanted to know Edwards' views – Edwards had made no secret of his opposition to the merger. During the drive, Kearton told Edwards that Leyland (which had recently altered its share capital) was prepared to make an opposed bid, and that, in Kearton's view, Leyland would win, thanks to the government and public opinion. In a newspaper interview, Stokes later confirmed that he had come close to launching an unwanted bid; but that this would have led to 'bitterness and trouble'. (Stokes had also asked James Slater, his former aide and now a powerful figure in the City, to draw up merger ideas.)

Edwards arrived at St James's where he found Stokes flanked by his financial advisers, Sir Siegmund Warburg and Sir Eric Roll, along with a partner from Cooper Brothers, the City accountants. Stokes asked Edwards whether he would accept the merger on the terms to which Harriman had agreed – which would make Stokes the supremo. A refusal would have raised serious problems, for Edwards had many backers on the BMC board. Edwards pondered, then said that he would accept; at the same time, he decided that he would leave British Leyland. Stokes had won.

Donald Stokes now held a position of great power and importance in British and international industry. His first step was to set up a network of study groups, with the twin aims of providing him with accurate, up-to-date information and of getting the two managements to get to know each other. Stokes flung himself into the reshaping: 'If you just want a central planner who sits and thinks round the coffee tables you've come to the wrong man.' What was Stokes' plan?

Short Term Savings

His immediate aim was to look for quick, short term savings while putting the group in a position for successful long term expansion. Among immediate savings, the most striking came from a drastic pruning of the model line which in a matter of months lost eighteen of its less profitable marques, ranging from the Princess and the MG Magnette down to less popular versions of the 1100. Stokes had been a persistent critic of BMC's badge engineering, and shortly afterwards took the further decision to axe one of BMC's best known names, Riley. The other immediate area for saving lay in the rationalization of overseas distribution, where Stokes had already had successful experience with Triumph and Rover. Local operations were merged into a single British Leyland network, and in markets like Australia and New Zealand where assembly operations were already established, co-ordination brought further savings in locally bought parts. In Europe, one of British Leyland's major growth areas, the problems were more difficult. Apart from an agreement with Innocenti in Italy, BMC had placed distribution in the hands of local dealers. British Leyland began a long drawn out, and at times painful, process of buying out their European distributors. In Britain, Stokes avoided the often urged plan of rationalizing BMC's dealer network with its 4500 organizations, of whom a quarter sold less than twenty cars a year. He argued: 'If you integrate, you must lose,' for the BMC network, while strong in the countryside, needed expanding in the towns.

On the financial side, Stokes' aim was to make use of under-exploited bank credit, plus normal cash flow, along with an IRC loan, to build towards his target of £50 million a year of new fixed investment. This was not intended to create any new, green field sites, but to cut costs through the modernization of production lines.

The entire British Leyland organization was divided into seven key divisions, each with a chief executive responsible to Stokes. The divisions were:

(a) Volume car and light commercial vehicles;
(b) Pressed Steel Fisher;
(c) Trucks and buses;
(d) Specialist cars – Jaguar, Rover, and Triumph;
(e) General engineering and foundries;
(f) Construction and equipment;
(g) Overseas manufacturing interests.

This organization was further refined in mid 1970.

This further refinement, which was made public in mid August 1970, represented the final management structure for the British Leyland group. Lord Stokes, as chairman and managing director, was delegated by the board, with the specific authority as chief executive to manage British Leyland and to be 'personally responsible to the board for the profitable operation of the corporation'. British Leyland's production organization was recast into five operating units:

(a) Volume cars, the Austin-Morris group, including Pressed Steel Fisher;
(b) Specialist cars, including Jaguar, Rover, and Triumph;
(c) Trucks and buses;
(d) Special products, including construction equipment;
(e) British Leyland International.

The corporate central staff was also reshaped, with a director of engineering standards and research responsible to Lord Stokes, and a director of facilities planning also responsible to Stokes, with responsibilities for rationalization.

British Leyland took a major step towards giving its managers personal responsibility. The internal policy statement laid down:

As managers at all levels are personally responsible for the performance of their units, no committee or subsidiary board in Leyland has authority to take a decision. The only collective responsibility in the corporation, and therefore the only body which is authorised to take a collective decision is the corporation board. Otherwise all decisions will be taken by individuals.

Each of British Leyland's five new divisions was also given an advisory board, whose function was to account to Lord Stokes for performance. Much of British Leyland's future success will depend on the efficiency of this new functional organization.

Speaking in May 1968, when the merger took formal effect, Stokes said:

We want to have all our various plants making more and more the same sort of thing. This will give us economies in production. Getting the products right is priority number one. Secondly we have to get on with the marketing. Then backing all that up, we have to get our production facilities right. Any benefits the group will get must take two or three years to materialise.

Stokes also rejected any suggestion of redundancy.

Austin-Morris

Leyland had had considerable success with its range of cars, but it had never operated at big volume where success depends on price and, therefore, on cost control. It was soon clear that BMC's volume car side, Austin-Morris, was going to be the decisive test for the new group. Stokes appointed himself for a time as head of the new volume car division, which made up the main part of the old BMC. He appointed George Turnbull as his chief executive, and as chief engineer, Harry Webster, the former chief engineer of Standard Triumph. Joe Edwards had now left, and Sir Alec Issigonis moved up to director level, with retirement three years away.

One of the key papers in the early days was the *Agreement on Principles of Management*. This was signed by the two boards (including Joe Edwards before he resigned) in April 1968, a month before the formal merger. This unusual document, which was circulated to all top managers, set out how British Leyland was to be run. The group was to be a 'single commercial organization', not a holding company with subsidiaries. It was to be run not by its board, but by the chief executive, Donald Stokes, who was responsible to the board and had below him line managers with clearly defined individual responsibilities plus small head office staff. This document set out the aims of the merger:

38

(*a*) Organization, to agree a proper divisional structure and to allot jobs;
(*b*) Model policy;
(*c*) In the light of these decisions, tackle the long term rationalization of production facilities and the dealer network.

That first year of the merger, starting in early 1968, saw the new team coping with a host of problems. BMC had built a modern commercial vehicle plant at Bathgate in Scotland, but this was making heavy losses and so was placed under the overall direction of Leyland-Albion. (Labour troubles multiplied at Bathgate, and at one stage the management had to threaten to close the entire plant. The flop of BMC's mini-tractor added to Bathgate's problems, and even ten years after it opened, the factory had not reached its initial production target of 1000 trucks and 750 tractors a week.) In South Africa, a neat and profitable swap was carried through, with BMC's truck production moved into Leyland factories and the manufacture of Triumph cars into BMC plants; similar moves were put under way in Australia.

At home, there was undeniably great scope for rationalization and tidying up – a job which fell largely to three ex-Ford men, Bert Walling, who was made overlord of purchasing; George King, production controller; and Filmer Paradise, sales director. British Leyland's central organization was also developed. One early exercise threw up the startling fact that BMC alone was spending £2·1 million a year on stationery and printing, divided between 300 suppliers. These were reduced to three with a saving of £150 000 a year.

Walling found he had inherited 42 purchasing offices within the corporation, of which 12 were within BMC and attached to individual companies rather than products. In this way many bought one product; no less than 31 still bought forgings. By similar rules, the corporation had as many as 36 paint suppliers, who provided no less than four distinct shades of black. BMC had a well established rule, for example, of one supplier of components for each model; this was reversed by Leyland so that Dunlop, for example, lost its exclusive position as supplier of tyres for Austin-Morris.

1500 Problems

Many of the merger problems, in the eyes of the new team, were reflected in the history of the 1500, the car designed to fill the gap between the 1100, which was launched in 1963, and the rather less successful 1800. Back in 1965, the 1500 was planned, and in May that year Sir George Harriman stated: 'We have to replace our 1500's in time.' (He was referring to the Oxford-Cambridge range.) In the same year, BMC launched a major expansion, spending £40 million on new plant and £10 million on modernization. In all this, the engine plant at Cofton Hackett, costing £16 million, played a key role. Joe Edwards' appointment as managing director of BMC in June 1966 had a major effect on the 1500. Edwards drastically, and rightly, modified its original engineering-based concept towards new ideas of market research and product planning. Heavy inroads made by the Ford Cortina into BMC's product range during 1966 against the ageing Austin Cambridge and Morris Oxford, played a major part in BMC's fall in market share, which in turn led to the laying-off of 12 000 men and to the financial problems of the following year. The 1500 had originally been planned for the 1967 Motor Show, and when the merger took place BMC still believed that it would be ready for the 1968 Show. But Stokes ordered further modifications and the car, delayed by a dispute over piece rates, did not appear until the following year.

British Leyland's first set of profit figures, issued almost exactly a year after the merger, received a warm reception in the City. Combined sales of £973 million produced profits of £38 million. But evidence mounted steadily that the volume car side of the group, Austin-Morris, contained the key to the eventual success of the merger, and that the progress of this division depended essentially on the group's labour relations policy. Even the 1968 recovery contained some disturbing pointers for BMC's model range. During 1967, sales of the Mini dropped by some 9000 and those of the 1100 and 1300 by 20 000; the 1600 range showed a fall of some 14 000 units. Most of the recovery by the volume car division the following year came from the 1100 and 1300 range and from a modest recovery by Mini sales. The 1600 series showed a further decline, while the 1800 and three litre group fell back even below the 1966–67 level.

In 1967, BMC held 42 per cent of the domestic market against Ford's 25 per cent. In May 1968, for the first time ever, Ford narrowly overtook BMC with around 29 per cent. This was regarded as 'a striking vindication of Ford's approach and a damning of BMC's'. Since then, British Leyland has held a lead over Ford, in a market where imports have become of major significance. BMC's commercial vehicles, which had been modelled on those of Bedford, had seen their market share drop from 20 per cent to 10 per cent.

Labour relations emerged as the key factor which was dominating the merger. Several years before, Joe Edwards had suggested to Harriman that Sir Jack Scamp, who had done useful work for the Motor Industry Joint Council, should be made director of labour relations. But the proposal broke down because Harriman was not then willing to give a labour director a seat on the main board. After the merger, Stokes asked Edwards if he would again approach Scamp to become labour director for the new group, but Scamp was by then committed. Early in 1970, Stokes appointed Pat Lowry, director of the Engineering Employers Federation, as director of industrial relations. Lowry, who had spent his entire working career with the Federation, was best known for negotiating consecutive three-year package deals with the country's engineering workers.

Stokes himself, in his maiden speech in the House of Lords on 5 November,

40

had underlined the importance of Lowry's appointment. But for industrial disputes, Stokes told the Lords, British Leyland could in 1968 have produced 100 000 more cars, at least 50 000 of which could have gone to export and have earned more than £26 million towards Britain's balance of payments.

Strike Losses

Throughout the winter of 1969–70, industrial relations throughout the entire British engineering industry grew steadily worse. The number of days lost climbed steadily, there was a proliferation of unofficial stoppages, with serious effects in such an interdependent industry; many of the disputes, including some of those made official, seemed to the outside world to be minor difficulties. As often happens in industrial relations, the particular dispute seemed to be the occasion, rather than the cause, of differences. By early 1970, Stokes estimated that his group had had only three days of entirely strike free production, since its formation in early 1968. At British Leyland's annual meeting in February 1970, Stokes launched a violent attack on the industrial anarchists who, he said, had been preventing the majority of their shop-floor colleagues from working. Revealing that the group had made no profit during the first four months of its financial year, Stokes underlined the warning of the dangers that lay in the government's refusal to ease the credit squeeze before the Budget. During the early months of the merger company, Stokes himself had played a major role in labour negotiations; by early 1970, these posed an acute dilemma for the British Leyland management. With whom should it negotiate? With the unions, who were often unable to control their men? With the shop stewards, who often wielded considerable power but whose growth could be dangerous for the future and unpopular with the unions? Or direct with the men themselves, which would be resented by the unions and shop stewards alike? Stokes' warning came just after Vauxhall had revealed its worst ever figures: a £2 million loss thanks to a bad year of labour disputes. (Vauxhall's succeeding half year figures were to prove even worse.) But Stokes faced a difficult problem. Labour relations in BMC had been particularly bad since the sacking of 12 000 workers in September 1966 as part of the efforts of the former management to cope with a serious fall in sales. The effect of this sacking, predictably, was to worsen overall labour relations and to reduce the productivity of the remaining 94 000 workers. Stokes' immediate concern, on gaining control, was to improve productivity. In early 1968, he therefore guaranteed that there would be no closing of factories in the immediate future. Stokes' hope had been that after a year, with improving productivity and profits, he would be able to rationalize the seventy plants which he had inherited. But the deterioration in labour relations became so bad that he was unable to carry out even the rationalization of three particularly out-of-date factories whose shutdown had been planned by the former BMC management. A strike at Leyland's own factory, which had until then enjoyed a particularly good labour record, attracted a great deal of attention. This was a further symptom of the attempted levelling up of wage rates to the Midlands level from which both BMC and Rootes had previously suffered; Leyland's productivity per man in Lancashire was lower than that in the Midlands, hence the lower wages, but this was not an argument calculated to appeal to the workers in Leyland, for whom the national process of leap-frogging promised useful cash benefits.

By the autumn of 1970, Pat Lowry had secured endorsement, by the British Leyland board, of a policy statement on labour relations. When he came to British Leyland, Lowry found wide differences in wages and bargaining procedures. His policy was based on two major assumptions. The first was that industrial relations had undergone a major change, in that workers demanded more than just adequate pay, and that previous authoritarian relationships could no longer survive. His second assumption was that the differential between white and blue collar workers should be reduced, particularly to remedy the lack of security for blue collar workers; lay-off pay, pay for lay-offs caused by outside disputes, emerged as one controversial point with the unions.

Piecework System

Lowry's besetting problem was the widespread piecework system throughout the British Leyland group, though some plants, such as Llanelly, did operate measured day work. Lowry aimed to put his plan into effect over about two years: a difficult part of his job was to establish a redundancy policy, which centred on the volume car side of British Leyland, through the merger of Austin-Morris with Pressed Steel Fisher. But redundancy was inevitably more complicated for British Leyland than, say, for GEC. British Leyland operated a large number of interdependent factories, so that redundancies depended to an important extent on model policy.

But new plants did give Lowry a chance to show what British Leyland aimed to do, as at the Workington bus factory, due to be commissioned in the spring of 1971. There the work force was divided simply into three grades: senior management, junior management, and a comprehensive factory floor group. At Workington, steps were taken to reduce the hierarchy which had grown up in older factories, down to differentiated car parks and canteens.

Leyland's results for the six months to March, which were published about three months after Stokes' speech at the annual meeting, underlined his warnings. Sales of £458 milllion reflected a drop in units produced, from 474 000 to 448 000, almost entirely because of industrial disputes. But the sensational figure was the size of British Leyland's profits – a mere £1·1 million compared to £19·3 million in the first six months of the previous year. After allowing for taxation and outside interests, BLMC was left with just £100 000; in effect,

42

this major industrial group had been working for six months and making virtually no profit. And during these six months, the group had lost 77 000 cars and commercial vehicles through industrial disputes, a significant deterioration on the already disturbing figures of the previous year. These 'lost' cars helped to swell the demand for foreign cars, which reached a striking 15 per cent of the total market by early 1970, in spite of their substantial tax and tariff disadvantage.

At this stage, Stokes had come to believe, with considerable justification, that labour problems had largely frustrated the aims of the merger itself. Above all, negating the policy of no closures and no massive redundancies on which the merger was based. Stokes later conceded: 'When we announced and agreed the Leyland-BMC merger, I said that we had several difficult years ahead. This has proved even truer than I thought . . .' British Leyland had become the focus for the problems of the British engineering industry: wage costs rising far ahead of productivity, especially from 1969 onwards, and above all, the critical problem of industrial disputes. The first major series of redundancies, involving 5000 men in the Austin-Morris division, was announced at the end of 1970.

The motor industry is essentially a moderately capital-intensive, assembly business, which depends for its efficient functioning on a large number, often several hundreds, of outside suppliers. In a large scale unit like Austin-Morris, output can be stopped or seriously slowed down by industrial disputes at any of the many stages culminating in final assembly. Thus a Pilkington strike stopped delivery of windscreens; a Wilmot-Breeden dispute stopped the flow of door locks and car bumpers; a strike at Adwest cut down supplies of power steering gear; a Lucas strike stopped delivery of starter motors; and so on. It was, reportedly, the ability of twenty-three apprentices at Girling's brake factory to hold up car production which convinced Mr Wilson, when he was Prime Minister, of the need for an industrial relations bill. On top of all this, British Leyland suffered its share of disputes within its own factories, which sometimes drew on surprising sources of support, such as left-wing Oxford undergraduates handing out leaflets in British Leyland's Cowley works.

Anarchy and Chaos

All this helps to explain why British Leyland was so vulnerable to the effects of industrial disputes. But it still leaves unanswered the question why such disputes arose – except to the extent that shop-floor workers in the motor and component industries must realize their considerable power. British Leyland was not suffering from some peculiar difficulty, but from a general affliction of the manufacturing industry: one of the ominous signs of the strike figures, especially during the first part of 1970, was how disputes had spread. In early 1970, Stokes warned British Leyland shareholders of 'anarchy and chaos' in the industry, a statement which brought claims of exaggeration. Six months later, he claimed: 'I feel that my words have been more than fully justified.'

To assess the broad industrial reasons for the spread of disputes, one needs to look beyond British Leyland and the motor industry as a whole. But it is clear that the success of British Leyland must depend on some solution being found to the principal industrial problems: the relating of wages more closely to productivity and above all the restraint of industrial disputes both official, and more especially, unofficial.

The second major condition for the success of British Leyland lies in its ability to compete both with the big three multinational producers and with the aggressive, nationally based groups of Western Europe and Japan. The merger of Leyland with BMC created a group with the capacity to produce 1 million units a year, often regarded as the minimum for viable independence. But British Leyland is unique in Europe in having to fight all three of the major US car producers in its own home market. Unlike Fiat, it does not hold the dominant position in its home market, and unlike Volkswagen it does not have a major place in one of the world's leading overseas markets. The problems of size and international growth are closely linked together: production ties with a European manufacturer would give British Leyland larger capacity and access to a wider market. Further tie-ups between Europe's native car producers are likely, especially as Britain moves towards membership of the EEC. There is also the prospect of car makers in Europe and the US tying up with the fast growing and aggressive Japanese car industry.

Many criticisms, both before and since the creation of British Leyland, have been directed against the old BMC management. But probably the most serious, from a long term view, was its inability in the 'sixties to turn what was Britain's biggest car producer into an international group. All the US car manufacturers saw the coming of internationalization of the car market: GM developed Opel and Vauxhall, Ford bought complete control in Britain, Chrysler bought control of Simca, then Barreiros, and finally Rootes. Volkswagen turned its people's car into a second car for the wealthiest nation in the world; Fiat spread its efficient sales network across Europe; and Citroen pushed into third place in the German car market. BMC was left behind. The British group held a strong place in the old Commonwealth, Australia, South Africa, and India, though its market share was eroded by US, European, and later Japanese, competition. But in Europe, BMC had managed only limited assembly agreements with Innocenti in Italy, who was not one of the major vehicle producers, and in Spain and Belgium. In the US, BMC did not attempt to sell saloon cars on any scale, but concentrated on sports models with useful, but necessarily limited, success.

The creation of British Leyland was clearly necessary if Britain wished to

44

retain an independent, national motor vehicle industry. But British Leyland in many ways poses all the problems of the British economy. Set up on a world or at least on a European scale, the group needs to maintain an adequate share of its domestic market while carving out larger business overseas. British Leyland, therefore, has to succeed in two ways: first, to achieve a competitive cost structure, which at the very least means a wages-productivity ratio and a disputes record which is no worse than that of its principal competitors. Second, British Leyland has to grow on a scale and with sufficient geographical diversity to match its US and EEC rivals and to gain from the expansion of new markets in Europe and elsewhere. That will be a major test for British Leyland in the 'seventies; in a real sense, it will also be a test of Britain as a major industrial power.

Rise and Fall of IPC

In his autobiography, *Strictly Personal*, Cecil King describes how, as chairman of the International Publishing Corporation, he engineered a £37 million bid for Odhams Press. King had approached Christopher Chancellor, then chairman of Odhams, to suggest a merger; Chancellor, however, preferred a merger with the Thomson Organisation. King relates how he watched Lord Thomson and Christopher Chancellor announcing their plans on television: '. . . I reached for the telephone, alerted my colleagues, and in fact we made a successful counter-bid.' By any standards, this was a major industrial deal. It brought with it the seeds of King's own dismissal from IPC and, to a large degree, IPC's own eventual loss of independence.

Odhams covered a large number of women's and consumer magazines, a market which was just beginning to decline, and whose alliance to IPC's existing Fleetway group needed a massive market-oriented rationalization in order to make it successful. Odhams also included two newspapers, *The People* and the *Daily Herald*. King's pledges to continue to publish the *Daily Herald*, later relaunched as the *Sun*, were eventually to cost IPC more than £12 million. King's pledge may well have been made to soothe the fears of the Labour Party.

IPC's directors may perhaps have been influenced by the obvious financial success of their takeover of Amalgamated Press for £16 million just two years before in 1959. 'Financially the purchase proved a bonanza for us,' King wrote later. This view was certainly justified: the value of the two subsidiaries, Imperial Paper Mills and Kelly-Iliffe, was greater than the price which IPC had paid for the entire group. In simple financial terms, this meant that the entire magazine part of the business, whose profits reached more than £1 million a year, had been acquired for free. The acquisition of Amalgamated Press also brought with it printing works whose problems were considerable, but which were not to become apparent for some time ahead.

When IPC was created, by the merger of the *Daily Mirror* with the *Sunday Pictorial* in 1963 (until then, the two groups had held cross shareholdings

46

in each other), IPC became the world's largest communications group. But like so many other mergers which were created during the 'fifties and 'sixties, IPC remained a conglomerate of largely independent companies. In other industries, the consequences of such a faulty structure were avoided or at least camouflaged by expansion, but IPC had to face a whole range of problems: the ending of the growth years for women's magazines; the growing problems of Fleet Street and particularly of the *Sun*, as advertising grew slowly with the economy, and as circulation was held back by television competition, while wage costs rose fast; and a major drain on profits and management time imposed by the two dozen printing works which the Corporation had inherited.

All this, of course, comes with hindsight. At that time, the early 'sixties, it was not clear that the magazines needed to be shaped into market-directed sections: women's interest, teenager interest, sport, and so on, rather than being left to individual companies. Indeed, after the takeover of Odhams in 1961, IPC shares became acceptable for the first time on a large scale to the major institutions in the City, who had for many years been deterred from investing in a left-wing communications-based group. The first public impression that all might not be well with the strategy of IPC came with the relaunch of the *Daily Herald* as the *Sun* in 1964. The *Daily Herald*, with its rather elderly working class and lower middle class readership, had faced declining advertising revenues and dwindling circulation. The relaunch following Cecil King's pledge, was accompanied by a major editorial face-lift and what was by Fleet Street standards an expensive, £400 000 publicity budget. Although 3 million copies were actually printed on the launch day of the new *Sun*, circulation revived only briefly to just over 1·3 million, and then went into a steady decline. By the latter half of 1968, the *Sun* was selling barely 1 million copies, and closure at that point was held back only by the undertaking to publish 'into the' seventies'. IPC's commitment to maintain the *Sun* could be justified on social grounds, particularly the identification of IPC with the Labour Party. The pledge may also have made it somewhat easier for IPC to streamline its printing works and to reduce overmanning on its other newspapers. The IPC board may also have been optimistic about the future trends of profits from the *Sun*. But by the late 'sixties, losses, running at £1 million a year and more, were too great to live with. IPC might have been able to cope with the difficulties raised by the *Sun*, but for other problems which began to loom from the mid 'sixties. Profits from printing virtually disappeared during 1965 and turned into losses during the following years. Magazine earnings, which had reached a peak of £5 million in 1965, then began to slide slowly downwards. The *Sun*'s losses were reflected in the figures recorded by Odhams Newspapers, which steadily showed losses from 1965 to 1968 and broke even in 1969, when the £1·25 million lost by the *Sun* was almost exactly offset by a similar profit earned by *The People*.

c

King's Departure

From 1966 to 1968, IPC profits rose to just over £12 million, but then fell back. One City analysis put the point that over that period all that the directors had to show for a 25 per cent increase in capital employed was a £3 million drop in before tax profits. In 1968 all the difficulties were brought together: profits from printing and publishing dropped from £10·8 million to £7·2 million; the Reed Paper group, in which IPC held a 27 per cent stake, cut its dividend; and IPC shareholders' own dividend was reduced from 21 per cent to 18 per cent. Moreover, in May, Cecil King abruptly departed as chairman, and was replaced by Hugh Cudlipp.

In a trading group, this position would have been difficult enough, but IPC's position was made more vulnerable by its large holdings of investments, notably in the Reed group, which was the largest, in Associated Television, British Relay Wireless, Cahners of the US, and others. During the latter part of 1969, for example, these investments represented about £50 million out of a total stock market capitalization of £100 million for IPC as a whole. This situation prompted many amateur takeover experts to do a simple sum. One could buy IPC for a premium above the market price, it was suggested, sell off the investments, realize ruthlessly other assets and properties and be left with control of say the *Daily Mirror* and the *Sunday Mirror* for very little. This piece of arithmetic or a variant of it had appealed to at least one famous takeover bidder during the late 'fifties. The IPC directors took these inquiries sufficiently seriously to contact major institutional holders in order to make sure that the board could rely on their support. IPC's vulnerability might well have been even greater during these years but for the Monopolies and Mergers Act of 1965. This piece of Labour legislation laid down that any merger between newspaper groups above a certain modest minimum circulation had to be referred to the Monopolies Commission. In all other cases, the Board of Trade could decide whether or not to refer the proposed merger; but in a newspaper merger, a reference was mandatory. In other words, any attempt by a newspaper group to win control of IPC, either in a friendly or unwanted takeover, would inevitably lead to a hearing by the Monopolies Commission.

The turning-point in IPC's history was May 1968 when Cecil King, who had been the architect of the group, was deposed as chairman and (by a quirk of the company's articles) also as a director. The most widely circulated reason for King's departure, a unanimous board decision, was his growing involvement in public affairs, particularly his criticism of the Wilson Government, a policy which left the *Daily Mirror* with critics on the left, yet without attracting friends from the right. This contrasted with the wartime and early postwar years when the *Daily Mirror* had been aggressively pro-Labour. But underlying King's departure were the poor financial results for 1968 and, above all, what appeared to be a persistent refusal, in the eyes of the board, to agree to the divisionalization of IPC in order to give it a modern corporate structure.

Management control of IPC for the following two years rested with three men: Hugh Cudlipp, the chairman, Frank Rogers, the managing director, and Gordon Cartwright, the finance director. The story of IPC rested on their, ultimately abandoned, efforts to keep the group independent.

McKinsey Structure

To assist in the divisionalization, IPC directors called in the US management consultants, McKinsey, to devise a new organization structure and to reshape the magazine side by market rather than by the accident of company ownership. Some tentative steps were also taken to develop the massive latent marketing power of the *Daily Mirror*, by forming associations with a holiday tours company and a unit trust management group. But there were two major areas on which the three new heads of IPC concentrated for improved financial results; these were the *Sun* and the large, loss-making printing side. IPC had a commitment to print the *Sun* 'into the 'seventies'. This was taken, reasonably enough, at its face value by the new board, and a closure was planned for 1970. The arithmetic of closure looked simple; to stop printing the *Sun* would end losses of £1·5 million a year, while a redundancy cost of some £2 million would be offset by having some £3 million of vacant buildings left for development.

On this basis, closure was irresistible, but there were two difficulties, one tactical and one strategic. The tactical difficulty was that *The People* and the *Sun* were printed on the same presses; if *The People* had to carry the entire overheads, its own profit would disappear. The obvious solution was to have *The People* printed by Associated Newspapers, who did not own a Sunday newspaper. But the negotiations had to be handled carefully, for the bargaining power in that situation clearly lay with Associated Newspapers.

The strategic question was to ensure that while the *Sun* remained in existence, it did not fall into the hands of a group which could develop it so as to damage the other newspaper interests of IPC; there was political and social pressure against killing the newspaper. The original solution was that Robert Maxwell, the chairman and controlling shareholder of Pergamon Press, would relaunch the *Sun* as a small circulation, high cost paper devoted to Labour Party politics. That would have brought a minimum loss of circulation to the *Daily Mirror*. Unfortunately, both for Maxwell and for IPC, this deal collapsed. All the problems caused by Leasco's attempt to bid for Pergamon Press, which monopolized the headlines during the late summer of 1969, compelled Maxwell to withdraw. The *Sun* was then sold to Rupert Murdoch, who negotiated a relatively attractive manning agreement with the unions, and relaunched the *Sun* as a popular tabloid. Though the *Sun*'s circulation was well under a third of that of the *Daily Mirror*, the new *Sun* took some readers from the *Daily Sketch* and a number from the *Daily Mirror* itself. From a long term point of view, therefore, IPC's closing of the *Sun* had not worked out happily. The effect of the decision had been, in effect, to put a newspaper group into the popular tabloid business.

The new IPC board's other tactical problem lay in the printing side, which employed about 7500 men and £20 million of capital, and which had lost £8 million over the four years to 1969. Cudlipp, Rogers, and Cartwright believed that the bulk of closures was behind them (including such large plants as Odhams at Long Acre and Cornwall Press in London), and that losses would turn to profits, particularly as IPC moved more of its own publication work, which had previously gone outside, into its own units. (This, incidentally, had been another source of contention under King's chairmanship. He had laid down that the magazines should have the cheapest and most suitable form of printing, even if this involved going outside IPC.) By mid 1969, Cudlipp and his colleagues hoped that the printing side could be contained at a much reduced loss the following year, and that over the subsequent two to three years, it would gradually make a profit. There again, their hopes of improvement were disappointed. Wage costs rose throughout the printing industry far ahead of productivity, industrial disputes became more widespread, and it soon became clear that IPC's printing side would need further managerial surgery.

Aubrey Jones Joins

The strategy of the IPC board in mid 1969 was roughly as follows: they took the view that IPC's existing interests contained sufficient profit potential to carry the group into the mid 'seventies, and that the major question was to decide where IPC should move beyond that time. Cudlipp saw this as his major task, and to help to resolve it he recruited Aubrey Jones, who was coming to the end of his term as chairman of the Prices and Incomes Board. Jones was to be an executive director and non-executive deputy chairman. (Rogers remained, of course, managing director of IPC), and his job in essence was to guide IPC towards the late 'seventies, by entering new fields: data and information retrieval, new types of communications, and so on.

This strategy depended for its credibility on the thesis that profits from existing interests would show sufficient growth during the intervening years. Even by mid 1969, it was clear that this strategy had its risks, for that year's profits were heading downwards. Earnings from newspapers were falling; wage and newsprint costs had risen while selling prices had remained static and advertising revenue showed little increase. IPC's printing division had moved further into the red, after an early improvement, while new developments, such as computer-based financial data production (intended to pave the way for new vistas in the mid 'seventies), were losing money. All of this might still have been sustainable but for a major new decision by IPC's newspaper side to launch a colour magazine in September 1969. The broad strategy of the decision was to place colour before the *Daily Mirror* readers before the ownership of colour television sets became widespread. The IPC board aimed to keep production costs down by using existing unutilized capacity at Watford. But advertisers who wanted to reach the *Daily Mirror*'s market were not ready for colour, and it was soon evident that the *Daily Mirror* had launched its colour magazine just at the time when consumer advertising was moving downwards, under the pressure of fiscal and monetary deflation. Even initial advertising bookings were poor and the magazine was soon appearing at an annual loss, and well short of its advertising targets.

By late 1969, therefore, the IPC directors were feeling anything but happy. They had expected a minor profit setback, but this had been made much worse by general economic conditions and by the bitterly disappointing launch of the *Daily Mirror* colour magazine. On top of all this, the necessary parting with the *Sun* had not worked out to IPC's best advantage. Short term profits provided the key to the IPC board's thinking; if profits for 1969–70 turned out reasonably well, their strategy might well command authority. If not, IPC could be subject to all kinds of external action ranging from pressure by larger sharholders to an outright takeover bid. The Monopolies and Merger Act would keep out an unwanted newspaper group, and a bid from abroad, for example, from one of the US entertainment conglomerates, might not find favour in Westminster, which was now better disposed towards IPC.

Given that short term profits were one of the key issues, IPC could have greatly improved its position by raising the price of the *Daily Mirror*, say sometime during the last quarter of 1969. But this would have raised great difficulties. The *Daily Mirror*, in process of losing some readers to the *Sun* (official estimates conceded 100 000, but the effective total was probably somewhat higher), could hardly risk a price increase ahead of the *Daily Express* and the *Daily Mail*. Moreover, IPC had keen memories of the previous series of price rises, when the *Daily Mirror* had led the way and run into difficulties with distributors.

The enigma to the outside world lay in the attitude of the IPC board, above all of the chairman, Hugh Cudlipp. 'A very good first violin but not a conductor' was how Cecil King had tartly described Cudlipp at the 1968 annual meeting, shortly after Cudlipp had led the coup which involved King's dismissal. Cudlipp seems, up to a degree at least, to have accepted King's remark: he later described his endorsement of the IPC takeover as 'handing over my Stradivarius'. Musical metaphors aside, the City was wondering, in the closing weeks of 1969, whether Cudlipp and his two most senior colleagues had the will to reorganize IPC in the way necessary to maintain its independence.

New Man Needed

The thinking of the IPC board, or at least of the three leading members, seems to have crystallized by the end of 1969 on the need for a ruthless chief executive who would carry through all the restructuring and pruning that was needed. Cudlipp seems never to have fully committed himself, as chairman, to this kind of role. Though the top trio seem to have accepted that either individually or collectively, they must take over this function. What seems to have destroyed their will to stay independent and take over these functions was the steady deterioration in IPC's profits, once the colour magazine moved into heavy deficit from September onwards.

What also influenced the IPC directors, above all Hugh Cudlipp, was that on the IPC board was a man clearly fitted for this tough chief executive role, Sydney Thomas Ryder. Don Ryder, as he is universally known, was then fifty-three, with an impressive career based solely on ability. His early ambition to become a financial journalist took him from school in Ealing to the *Morning Post*. After the Second World War, he returned to journalism and in 1950 became editor of the *Stock Exchange Gazette*. During these years, Ryder founded his reputation for toughness, professionalism and, above all, for prodigious hard work. Ryder's big chance came in 1960, when he toured with Cecil King in Canada. Ryder excelled at memorizing names and anticipating problems. A tour with King was by no means an assurance of promotion. Ryder himself later pointed out: 'A lot of people went on trips with him and came back pretty damned quickly . . .' The story goes that King asked Ryder, in a general conversation, how he would deal with the problems of Kelly-Iliffe which had come to IPC through Amalgamated Press. Ryder's reply, it is said, was to hand King a detailed memorandum.

On his return, King nominated Ryder as chief executive of Kelly-Iliffe, where he virtually doubled profits in three years. This achievement brought Ryder a seat on the main IPC board, just in time for his next, and biggest, opportunity. IPC then held a 44 per cent share interest in Reed Paper, which ran into difficulties in 1963. Cecil King abruptly took over the chair himself, and he named Ryder as managing director.

Ryder's reputation as a first rank industrialist rests on his success at Reed. Profits doubled, from £8·5 million in 1963 to £17 million in 1969, despite a sharp rise and fall in 1966–67 as a result of the seamen's strike, overcapacity in Canada, and increased Scandinavian competition. But Ryder's reputation was also built up on his skilful reshaping of the structure of the Reed group. Ryder carried through a massive reshuffling of the company in order to turn it into a consumer-directed organization. He proved skilful at picking new management talent. He was especially successful at integrating the big, family run Wall Paper Manufacturers, of which Reed won control after a sharply fought takeover battle.

By late 1969, Reed had outgrown IPC, its former major shareholder.

The acquisition of Wall Paper Manufacturers, following the takeover of Spicers, enlarged Reed and reduced IPC's share interest from 44 per cent to 27 per cent. After the problems of 1966–67, Reed had begun by 1968 to move out of its bad patch. The paper business began an upward trend, new paint brands proved successful, and the overseas side started to recover. Reed's revival added to Ryder's reputation.

Buying Management

During these years Reed paid £8 million or so for Field Sons and Co. of Bradford, a takeover which was very different from the usual bid by a large for a small group. When he took over executive control at Reed, Ryder found that the carton side – packets, from cigarettes to Daz – was losing money. He also discovered that other big companies were losing money on cartons. Further investigation showed that one public company could make money out of cartons – Field, a very efficient, highly respected company where the entire board worked in overalls. Ryder visited Field, not just with a takeover offer (these were no novelty to the Field board) but with the proposition that Reed would buy Field and give Field executives the running of Reed's entire carton business. The deal went through on this basis. Some Reed men may not have relished the introduction of outsiders, but the Field management succeeded in putting Reed's carton business on to a profitable basis.

Cecil King's departure from IPC precipitated Ryder's thinking for further expansion and he pressed for a merger with the Bowater Paper Corporation – a running theme in those years. Reed and Bowater enjoyed good trading relations (they co-operated, with IRC help, to take over Inveresk's mill at Donside), but the IPC board vetoed the plan. According to King, the IPC directors 'were afraid the merged Reed-Bowater company would make a bid for IPC'. Diverted from this idea, Ryder started to plan an even more far reaching international strategy. With Hoechst, the German chemical giant, Ryder worked out a scheme to give Reed scope for selling paint and wallpaper inside the Common Market. Hoechst, on its side, aimed to enter the British paint market, which led to a successful bid for Berger Jenson. Hoechst also sought outlets for plastics in Britain, as a complement to Reed's plans in Europe.

Invitation to Ryder

Just as these potentially far ranging ideas were nearing completion at Reed's headquarters, the IPC directors had come to accept that they should ask Ryder to take over IPC before an unwanted bidder came along. In the autumn of 1969, IPC appointed Arthur Winspear, a director of the merchant bankers SG Warburg, to its board. Warburgs had acted for IPC, as well as Reed, and outside financial advice would clearly be necessary. By the closing weeks of 1969, Cudlipp seems firmly to have decided that an invitation to

Ryder provided the only solution. He was backed by Gordon Cartwright, with some reservation about the terms, and by Frank Rogers who finally accepted that IPC needed to call on outside aid. The majority of the IPC board supported Cudlipp, but their views ranged from resigned acceptance to a few who opposed the idea. Paul Hamlyn, the ex-Bevin boy who had sold his highly successful publishing business to IPC, argued that the corporation could find its own salvation. Hamlyn was supported by Arnold Quick, chairman of IPC magazines.

Cudlipp received his mandate to invite Ryder into IPC and the final, very rapid series of talks began on 20 January 1970, when Cudlipp called at the Piccadilly headquarters of Reed. At short notice, merchant bankers, Kleinwort Benson, were asked to advise IPC. On the evening of Friday 23 January, the announcement was made public after stock market speculation that Courtaulds, the Rank Organization, or Slater Walker would make a bid. Once the decision had been reached, Ryder and Cudlipp pushed ahead. Senior IPC executives were told that evening, and Cudlipp held a lunch for his editors, at his favourite restaurant, the White Tower in Soho, the following day.

After the press conference on Friday evening at Reed's office, which was handled by Ryder with his usual skill, Ryder and Cudlipp made an important visit to 10 Downing Street. It would have been normal courtesy to inform the Prime Minister of such a deal, especially in view of Mr Wilson's particular interest in the press. But the essential point at issue lay in the safeguards which Reed was prepared to offer in order to maintain IPC newspapers' editorial independence. This was achieved by Cudlipp staying as chairman of IPC, while he also became one of the three deputy chairmen to Ryder in the merger group. Although the Reed-IPC merger escaped a mandatory reference to the Monopolies Commission (because Reed had no newspaper interests), the transaction could still have been referred by the Board of Trade under the rule which allowed it to refer any merger which involved more than £5 million. But support among Labour Ministers soon emerged for the view that, provided Ryder could offer adequate safeguards for the *Daily Mirror*'s editorial independence, a review by the Monopolies Commission would be time wasting and out of place.

When news of the Reed-IPC merger burst on the world that Friday night, the immediate reaction was to look for a counter-bid. Analysts in the City had been doing their sums over IPC, and these suggested that the Reed offer price could be improved. Paul Hamlyn, the IPC director who had argued that IPC could do for itself anything that Ryder could, stated in public over the weekend: 'People are doing their sums at this very moment. They may find they could pay a lot more for the group and still have a bargain.' A counter-bid depended either on an approach from another newspaper group, which would have involved a mandatory reference to the Monopolies Commission, or on a breaking up of IPC.

Bowater Ponders

But everyone first looked to Bowater House in Knightsbridge as the prime source of a counter-attack. During the following Sunday, Martin Ritchie, the energetic Scotsman who had succeeded Sir Christopher Chancellor as chairman of Bowater Paper, assembled his board for a day long meeting. Bowater was Reed's dominant rival in the paper business and commanded the resources to initiate a £100 million or more takeover. Bowater, being independent of any particular newspaper group, was well suited to initiate a consortium for a rival takeover.

There was an intriguing historical analogy; in 1961, when Cecil King had launched his bid for Odhams Press, there had also been talk of a consortium to plan a counter-offer. That consortium hinged on Bowater, but King was able to secure Bowater's neutrality by agreeing with the then chairman, the autocratic Sir Eric Bowater, that the new group would be a large customer. On that occasion, Sir Eric Bowater had decided, reasonably, that his prime interest lay in obtaining outlets for newsprint. Would Martin Ritchie do the same? The dangers to Bowater's situation were clear: the contracts which Cecil King had arranged with Sir Eric Bowater were running out, and Bowater could be squeezed out as a supplier if Don Ryder met IPC's demands from the surplus capacity of Reed's British mills and from Canada. Such a tactic would make clear sense for an integrated group and could have produced useful profits for Reed-IPC.

Throughout that Sunday, the Bowater directors pondered; they were assured by their bankers, Hill Samuel and N. M. Rothschild, that they had the resources to launch, or certainly to initiate, a counter-offer, but Ritchie took a different view from Sir Eric Bowater. In Ritchie's opinion, Bowater did not have the expertise to run, or to rationalize, a large section of the printing business as well as newspapers, the two operations which were essential for a revival of IPC. By the evening, the Bowater board had unanimously decided to take no action and Ritchie issued a statement that his company had no present intention of intervening in the Reed-IPC merger proposal, though he added that in the event of intervention by any other party, Bowater might have to think again.

Jim Slater, too, made clear over that weekend that he was 'not interested'. He had apparently come to believe that the possible financial attractions of a bid for IPC would be more than offset by the political difficulties he would face and by the peculiar problems of the printing and publishing industry.

But for the first week or so after the first news of the bid, Bowater's position remained crucial. Bowater supplied some 45 per cent of IPC's newsprint requirements, apart from coated paper for magazines which in turn represented between 20 per cent and 25 per cent of Bowater's total

55

newsprint output. Ritchie's public silence was based on his decision to seek by negotiation what Sir Eric Bowater had obtained by threatening war.

A series of talks between Ritchie and Ryder lasted the whole of the following week, mainly at the Pall Mall offices of the IRC. The IRC had already been involved with Reed and Bowater over Donside, and with Reed on a de-inking import-saving scheme. The IRC had been concerned about imports of newsprint following a 1967 report by the Prices and Incomes Board on newspaper prices. In the negotiations, Bowater held the strong position that any replacement of its supplies to IPC by imports from Canada would add to the country's import bill – in a situation where substantial imports were already combined with excess capacity in Britain. It was in Ryder's interest, too, to agree with Bowater. Not merely would an agreement eliminate the prime source of any consortium, but the support of Bowater would underline the industrial logic of the Reed-IPC merger; opposition from the industry might have made it difficult for Whitehall to avoid referring the affair to the Monopolies Commission. By the end of that week, Ritchie and Ryder, with Sir Joseph Lockwood, chairman of the IRC, had reached a three-point agreement. The agreement also ensured that the merger would not add to Britain's prevailing level of imports. The three-part agreement was as follows:

(a) IPC would continue to take nearly 60 per cent of its newsprint requirements from British mills, so long as other newspapers were not able to buy abroad at lower prices.

(b) Ryder agreed to support IRC and PIB attempts to persuade British newspapers to absorb the excess capacity in British mills. At the time, surplus capacity represented perhaps 80000 tons out of a total capacity of 830000 tons.

(c) Ryder agreed to limit Reed sales to the newspaper industry, assuming that the level of imports remained unchanged at the prevailing level of 185000 tons a year. That figure implied that Reed would be able to supply an extra 13000 tons to IPC, but that would represent the limit of its benefits from integration. Reed had made a significant sacrifice: before the merger it supplied IPC with some 50000 tons of newsprint from its British mills and rather more from its Canadian mills, against 110000 tons from Bowater.

Though this deal was blessed by the IRC and the Ministry of Technology, it was set aside finally by the DEP, partly it seems because of possible reactions from Scandinavian members of EFTA. Reed's only commitment now, it would seem, is simply that IPC should buy its newsprint at commercial prices.

Agreement with Bowater finally eliminated any political case for referring Reed-IPC to the Monopolies Commission. For the public interest, a reference to the Commission, or preferably to some speedier and more penetrating inquiry, might have been useful, but by the end of January both Whitehall and the newsprint industry believed that an inquiry was no longer necessary.

Three Dangers

From now on, all should have been plain sailing for Don Ryder, but he still faced dangers from three fronts. The first was the prospect of a takeover bid from a financial group who, by splitting up IPC, could make the shares worth more than the Reed bid. A number of plans for splitting IPC had been worked out, more or less informally, in the City in the months before Ryder appeared. The arithmetic was admittedly not quite as simple as it looked, for a plan to realize the investments and sell off properties would be matched by the problems of closing the printing side, and finally of finding a buyer at an acceptable price for the *Daily Mirror* and *Sunday Mirror*, the profitable heart of the publishing business. But there was no difficulty about methods (one course would have been to issue realization certificates) and the financing of such an operation was not beyond the means of some of the more aggressive financial groups. But there was one crucial question: the attitude of Whitehall. The Board of Trade could refer such a bid, which the IPC board would certainly resist, to the Monopolies Commission on grounds of asset size alone – even if the bidding did not include newspaper interests which would involve a mandatory reference. Discreet soundings were, therefore, taken in Westminster to establish what the government's attitude would be in the event of such a takeover approach. The answer was clear: the Wilson Government would not favour any takeover which involved a breaking up of IPC.

Don Ryder's problem was that a major industrial group might launch a counter-bid for IPC, one which would not involve any dismembering of the group and whose terms the IPC directors might find hard to refuse. The favourite candidate for this role was Courtaulds, the textile giant, whose paper and paint interests, it was suggested, would complement the consumer-oriented business of IPC. Lord Kearton was always extremely circumspect when taxed about his intentions but the rumours seem to have been fed by a remark he was said to have dropped at a cocktail party, that he was 'watching the situation with interest'.

Courtaulds' interest was real enough. An important medium term question for the group was how to deploy the large cash flow that was in prospect. For some time, the conventional wisdom at Courtaulds had been a future bid for Reed. The Reed-IPC takeover upset this thinking, but Courtaulds was apparently keen to make an offer for IPC. It believed that it could inject new life into IPC's magazines, though these drew a large part of their advertisement revenue from ICI, the leading rival of Courtaulds. IPC's newspaper side, it seems, was not of paramount interest to Courtaulds who thought of hiving off the *Daily Mirror* and other newspapers into a separate

57

organization. Courtaulds talked to Reed-IPC and also to Government Ministers. It did not receive much encouragement in Whitehall. Though Courtaulds had the resources to make an attractive bid for IPC, its expertise in communications was not obvious. More important, a bid by Courtaulds against Reed for IPC would probably have meant a reference to the Monopolies Commission – and during that time IPC's already difficult situation would have become much more serious. Ryder, reasonably enough, was not disposed to offer any concession to Courtaulds and made clear that Reed would not take part in a battle. Courtaulds pondered; the board authorized Lord Kearton to go ahead and terms were worked out. But finally Courtaulds decided to drop out; the size of the bid, the different nature of IPC's business, and the lack of enthusiasm in Whitehall seem to have induced Courtaulds to give up.

Whatever the source, rumours of Courtaulds' intervention proved so strong that there were heavy dealings in Reed shares around mid March, two weeks after the government had formally stated that it would not refer the merger to the Monopolies Commission. Don Ryder, when approached, could only say: 'I have heard many rumours, all of which I believe to be totally untrue.' There was little for Reed and its financial advisers to do but wait. The government decision not to refer came on 25 February, and the Reed offer did not close until 23 March. This allowed plenty of time for rumours and counter-rumours to develop.

The third source of problems for Ryder lay inside IPC itself. When the bid was first announced, opposition had been voiced by Paul Hamlyn and Arnold Quick. Quick had already announced his intentions to leave IPC, but Hamlyn remained a major shareholder. This public opposition seems to have stirred into action a small group of managers and writers, mainly within the magazine division, who tried to organize a pressure group to block the Reed bid. These 'rebels' took such care to seek refuge in anonymity that it is difficult to gauge how powerful a group they ever represented. But their main cause for complaint seems to have been that the IPC board had too readily handed over its independence. The rebels aimed to influence shareholders to reject the bid and to seek a saviour, assuming one were needed, elsewhere. One suggestion put forward by the rebels' spokesman was Sir Lew Grade, the chief executive of Associated Television; how seriously this was intended it is impossible to judge.

Terms Improved

The rebels were probably no more than a propaganda irritant to Ryder. Rather more serious were the reservations, put inside the IPC board by Hamlyn and Quick, and supported to a degree by other directors, that the bid price was not quite good enough. After the initial terms were announced, talks continued between the two sides about a possible revision and new terms were finally announced in the middle of the following month. The effect (at prevailing prices) was that Reed increased its offer for IPC by about £7 million to a total of £115 million. The details of the new terms were five Reed shares for every sixteen IPC ordinary shares plus £1·12½ worth of Reed unsecured loan stock. The effect on IPC shares was to make them worth 82p, compared with the original value of 85p which had dropped (following the fall in Reed shares) to 76p. For Reed, the revised terms involved the issuing of some £1 million fewer ordinary shares but nearly £10 million worth of unsecured loan stock. A formal statement on the revised offer merely referred, with utter obscurity, to 'a mutual exchange of information and subject to further examination certain aspects of this information'. More to the point, a special meeting of the IPC board was called on 18 February to endorse the new offer terms and the principle of the merger with Reed. Paul Hamlyn, who had become a focus of criticism of the Reed merger, now conceded that there was no viable alternative and urged that the improved terms be accepted.

The merger finally went through in early April and Ryder soon put into effect a new corporate structure – perhaps, as at Kelly-Iliffe, one which he had been planning for some time past. Four main groups were established: Reed Paper (paper, packaging, and converting); IPC (printing and publishing); Wall Paper Manufacturers (decorating and building materials); and Reed Overseas Corporation. Ryder was chairman, with three deputy chairmen, H. W. Broad, Hugh Cudlipp, and P. H. Sykes, responsible for finance, editorial, and technical fields respectively. Ryder lived up to his own declared philosophy: 'There is too little decision making . . . the important thing is to act.'

Ryder himself became chairman and chief executive of Reed International and chairman of each of the four divisions, apart from IPC of which Hugh Cudlipp took the chair. Ryder was also chairman of the executive committee of each of the four divisions, which at IPC did not include Hugh Cudlipp. Ryder himself put the management case for the merger:

> Over the years, IPC has helped Reed with the management. But we have now got to the stage where the quality of Reed management is very high, and unless we give our racehorses a race to run we would have to let them loose into other people's pastures.

Formal Approval

Formal approval from government involved three conditions: that the editorial freedom of the *Daily Mirror* be maintained; that in buying newsprint IPC would continue to be guided by commercial considerations; and that the copyright of Butterworth's legal books would stay in Britain. As Ryder himself made clear, the assurance of editorial freedom presented no problem, while on newsprint he stated: 'I am confident that this guarantee will not harm Reed.' The third element was designed to ensure that Halsbury's *Laws of England*, in particular, would not be taken over by a foreign group.

By an odd coincidence, Ryder had set out his management strategy only a few days before the IPC merger was announced, in a speech to the British Institute of Management. Ryder explained what he had set out to do at Reed. The company had entered the 'sixties as a paper producer and converter in an industry where profits had declined rapidly after the Korean War. An agreement for the removal of tariffs under the Stockholm Treaty of 1960 'threatened our very survival'. Reed had begun to adjust to this situation before Ryder took over as chief executive in 1963, but he launched into a far reaching, four-point plan:

(a) To expose the true position of the various parts of the company and management performance by decentralization;

(b) To change production dominance into market orientation;

(c) To achieve growth of profitability;

(d) To secure and develop professional managers.

An essential part of Ryder's programme was the management audit, designed to assess whether the right people were in the right jobs. This audit, he found, was hampered by the lack of criteria for measuring performance, since the results of Reed's various divisions had been clouded by shared services and common overheads. Ryder, in contrast, was a firm believer in management by objectives: 'I think that in a large diversified company the setting of objectives must be the best way for the group to control the many varied operating units.'

Perhaps it is only fair to leave Ryder himself with the last word. Presenting the first annual report of Reed after the takeover of IPC, he admitted that IPC contained areas of 'unacceptable losses' which 'must be remedied or removed'. He continued: 'I can assure you that the problems are being tackled vigorously and realistically.'

The full results of Ryder's policies at IPC, and, therefore, a final judgement on their success, must necessarily wait for several years. But Ryder's first major public move at IPC, announced in the summer of 1970, illustrates the size of the problems and Ryder's plans for their solution.

Ryder closed the *Daily Mirror* magazine, shut down one of Fleetway's major printing works, and laid down a tough, make-or-break schedule for IPC's new printing factory at Southwark. Ryder highlighted the magnitude of the problem which had induced Cudlipp and his board to give up independence:

Losses in certain areas of the company are being made at an annual rate of £6 million which is large enough to endanger the established profitable parts of the business and in total constitutes a serious threat to the whole organisation.

60

Management Mistakes

Equally succinctly Ryder explained why IPC 'so strong financially a few years ago' had come to this situation:

> Undoubtedly, there have been mistakes on the part of management. IPC in the course of its reorganisation has in my view over-reached itself in its attempts to diversify and find alternative areas of growth.

Three factors, in his view, had combined to turn these management mistakes into serious financial losses: first, material production costs, notably newsprint and ink had increased sharply; second, in the years of slow economic growth under the Wilson Government, above all after 1966, advertising expansion had fallen below the level of recent years; third, IPC had faced a series of problems on its labour side, productivity in the London printing works had failed to match rising wages, while a series of disputes had disrupted work and seriously affected the circulation of many periodicals. Few, if any, of these problems were peculiar to IPC. In fact, they all, especially the steep rise in wage costs, underlay the serious economic climate which confronted Fleet Street as a whole.

Characteristically, Ryder set out the full magnitude of the problems: the *Daily Mirror* magazine had been losing £30 000 a week in 1969–70 (apart from the launching costs), and was expected to lose a staggering £3 million in 1970–71. The cause of the magazine's death was clear: launched on the forecast of £7 million a year advertising revenue, it managed to reach no more than £4·5 million, and the bookings for the autumn of 1970 had fallen below even that reduced figure.

Printing in London, the other area which Ryder attacked, had lost IPC £1·36 million in 1969–70, with the bulk of the deficit concentrated at Fleetway's Sumner Street factory and at Southwark. In 1970–71, Ryder expected that the losses made by these two units alone would grow from £1·28 million to £1·75 million. The Southwark offset factory was in many ways a monument to the luddism of some Fleet Street printers. IPC built a new factory there in 1964, concentrating magazine printing in central London on the view that modern equipment plus a guaranteed turnover could create a viable unit. But the originally agreed manning levels and operating methods were never implemented. In 1967, the London printing unions, the Printing and Kindred Trades Federation, tried to carry through a new set of agreements, but these were rejected on the shop floor. Ryder conceded that the entire blame did not lie with the unions or even with their members, and put forward a scheme by which Southwark's losses would be cut from £1·2 million a year to £250 000 a year over three years. Ryder stated that the changes which were the only alternative to a complete shutdown, would be 'most painful' and would involve a 'considerable readjustment'.

These phrases, and Ryder's entire presentation of his mid 1970 plan, are wholly typical of his methods and approach: full presentation of relevant facts, objective analysis, and swift action. Ryder, like Weinstock, possesses such outstanding management qualities that large companies are attracted like planets round some new sun. IPC presents one of the very few cases where the board of a large company voluntarily agreed to surrender its independence – in circumstances where it could, admittedly with some difficulty, have maintained a separate existence for a considerable time to come. The action taken by Cudlipp, Rogers, and Cartwright is as much a reflection of Don Ryder's own qualities as of the problems which IPC itself was facing.

Blending Cadbury-Schweppes

Shortly after the French revolution, a certain Jacob Schweppe opened a factory in London to make high quality carbonated waters. Just over thirty years later, John Cadbury started a tea, coffee, and cocoa business in Birmingham. These two businesses came together in March 1969 when, in the largest merger of the year, Schweppes acquired the Cadbury business.

John Cadbury began making cocoa in 1831 and ran the business until 1860, when he was succeeded by his two sons Richard and George. They began selling pure cocoa and, in 1868, produced the first picture boxes of chocolates. In 1879, the brothers took the major step of buying the Bournville Estate, four miles outside Birmingham, where they built the Bournville factory and started the now famous garden suburb. Cadbury's Dairy Milk chocolate appeared shortly before the First World War, and just after, in 1919, Cadbury merged with J. S. Fry of Bristol, to form the British Cocoa and Chocolate Company. Between the wars, Cadbury developed overseas, opening seven new factories, all of them in the Commonwealth. Elsewhere, notably in the US, France, and Belgium, Cadbury set up marketing organizations, and at home bought a retail chain, R. S. McColl, based mainly in Scotland. A major new step for Cadbury came in 1962 when British Cocoa and Chocolate became quoted on the stock exchange, although family control remained. Two years later, Cadbury bought the Pascall and Murray confectionery firms from Beecham and diversified further into food products, notably cakes and groceries such as instant tea and mashed potatoes.

In Britain, meanwhile, Schweppes was building up a major position in the supply of carbonated (fizzy) drinks. Schweppes became firmly established as the major supplier to Britain's public houses and also concentrated on development abroad. A manufacturing plant was established in Australia shortly after the middle of the nineteenth century. After 1945, Schweppes was very much under the operational control of Sir Frederic Hooper, one of the earliest exponents in Britain of professional management. Sir Frederic, a vigorous and colourful figure, saw that Schweppes needed to diversify. Its dependence on public house trade offered limited growth, while the grocery business had come under considerable pressure from aggressive supermarket groups. Schweppes applied its marketing skills to Dubonnet, which proved one of the outstanding successes in the drink market of postwar Britain. It was the plan to diversify into the light consumer field that led Sir Frederic Hooper into jam, where he bought Hartley's, Moorhouse, and Chivers. These acquisitions brought useful advantages for Schweppes, notably by taking it further into the grocery trade, but jam sales in Britain were growing only slowly. These takeovers did not provide the financial take-off for which Sir Frederic and his colleagues had been seeking.

Schweppes grew fast, from profits of under £800 000 in 1952 to more than £5 million in 1966. Harold Watkinson, the former Conservative Minister, now Lord Watkinson, took over as group managing director on the death of Sir Frederic Hooper in 1963. When he assumed executive power, Watkinson found the group 'endeavouring to digest the somewhat large dose of diversification'. He regarded his initial task as consolidation, since he felt that the main board was 'creaking under the strain', and the business had reached the stage where it seemed unlikely that it could continue to be controlled by the managing director. Innovation in advertising had lagged behind, a new structure was needed for different markets; the overriding authority of the main board had been reduced; and senior executives concentrated too much on reporting known progress. Lord Watkinson in fact anticipated the market-oriented organization which was later to find favour among outside consultants. On the retirement of Hanning Philipps on 1 January 1969, Watkinson took over as chairman of Schweppes, and one of his first moves was to set up the overseas division. At home, he established two market-oriented divisions, one for the licensed and catering trades and the other for food. This reduced the effective management structure at home to four units: the main Schweppes' board and three operating divisions. Arthur D. Little was called in, because of its expertise with food companies, to investigate the Schweppes food division which embodied many of the latest acquisitions.

As chief executive of Schweppes, Lord Watkinson launched an important new move by taking over Typhoo Tea of Birmingham. The bid for Typhoo, announced in January 1968, was set under way the previous August, when Lord Watkinson was introduced to Henry Kelley, the Typhoo chairman and managing director. Typhoo did little overseas business, where Schweppes was extremely strong. Lord Watkinson explained that Schweppes had considered numerous other projects over the past year including Smiths Crisps, which was taken over by General Mills of the US just a month before the Typhoo deal. 'We can see great scope in development, particularly in the United States and other foreign markets.' The Typhoo directors, in supporting the bid, stated: 'Your board has been conscious for some time of the need of diversification' but they explained that the necessary diversification 'could not have been achieved on the basis of Typhoo's own resources'.

64

Rowntree–General Foods

Long term planning at Schweppes and Cadbury, and indeed throughout the whole food industry, moved into a new and more active phase with the determined, but finally unsuccessful, attempt made by General Foods to take over Rowntree. Rowntree had had only a moderately successful profit record; General Foods had developed marketing techniques in Britain, and had surplus capacity at their Banbury factory. The final decision, it was soon clear, was made by the Rowntree trustees, who held control of the company. A merger between Rowntree and Schweppes could have been a possibility, but this was ruled out by Schweppes' links with the drink trade. Despite successively improved offers from General Foods, the Rowntree trustees rejected its bid and carried through a merger with the confectionery firm of Mackintosh. The effect of this struggle was to underline the importance of mergers and the threat of US competition. Schweppes had set up a unit to investigate merger possibilities – and this unit had already suggested Typhoo. The same unit also pointed to Cadbury. A long and detailed study was produced which covered the total market for food and drink products in Britain, and also took account of overseas outlets. Development abroad played a major part in Schweppes planning: growth possibilities overseas were attractive, but Schweppes was limited by its financial resources. It suffered from the voluntary restraint on overseas investment; the refusal of the Treasury to sanction Schweppes' taking up shares in its Australian company could have meant that the London parent lost control.

While General Foods' attempt to take over Rowntree aroused a good deal of interest at Schweppes' Marble Arch headquarters, the attempted US invasion also sharpened thinking among the Cadbury directors at Bournville. They went into unscheduled session after news of the bid, announcing: 'This development is clearly of great importance to our industry, and naturally we are studying the situation.' Adrian Cadbury, who was told of the news while on a ski-ing holiday in Switzerland, flew back to head a further board meeting. Evidence of Cadbury's interest came from another quarter only a few days later when Charles Smith, chairman of the National Joint Industrial Council for the Chocolate and Cocoa Industry (whose members included a large number of Rowntree employees), said: 'I know Cadbury are interested and I think they will be able to come forward with a bid. It is an extremely good firm and I think it would benefit both companies.' Adrian Cadbury explained that his company had made no approach to Rowntree, but reaffirmed that: 'Obviously this is a matter of great interest to us.'

Cadbury faced a basic problem common to many major groups which had established a leading position in their industry. Over ten years, profits had moved barely £500 000 from the peak of £9·4 million before tax that had been achieved in 1957. The solution, engineered to a large degree by Adrian

Cadbury himself, was to look for new markets and to shape the large organization for a successful search. 'If we are to continue to grow we must look at ourselves not as a chocolate firm but as a food company.' On this basis, Cadbury moved into packaged cakes in 1962, and won a 9 per cent share of the market. Then came the pioneering and extremely successful launch of Marvel powdered milk, a mistaken venture into pre-packed meat (the cooked meat factory had to be closed in 1967), and other grocery products. In 1967, Cadbury carried through an outstandingly successful diversification, the launch of Smash instant potato. It was to help develop Cadbury's strategy that Adrian Cadbury, who became chairman at the age of thirty-six, called in the consultants, McKinsey. Adrian Cadbury himself was very much the centre of the organization, and combined, at one point, the posts of company chairman, chief executive, and general manager for the key confectionery division, which he described, rather charmingly, as 'going back to seventeenth-century pluralism, I am afraid, but only temporarily'. Cadbury himself wanted to handle delicate problems such as the confectionery side of Fry, whose separate traditions went back 200 years. Cadbury's problems were underlined by the pause in the share price; introduced at nearly £2·50 on the London Stock Exchange in 1962, the shares had difficulty maintaining that level. Cadbury was in effect immune to a takeover, except by agreement of the family and the board. But to grow, Cadbury needed to widen its interests and to enlarge its management techniques. When the merger plan with Schweppes was announced, it was clearly the new foods division which formed the major link between the two companies. Cadbury's set up, two years before the merger, included Smash, Marvel, cakes, and puddings with sales in the first year after formation of over £20 million. While Cadbury concentrated on the sweeter side of food, Schweppes, notably through the acquisition Harvey's of Belgravia (producer of the Duo-can), concentrated on delicatessen lines which married well with its drinks business.

Scope Overseas

Talks between Cadbury and Schweppes began in November 1968 and progressed fast. Overseas where, as Lord Watkinson explained, Schweppes' profits of £2·5 million in 1967 had doubled in the previous five years, possible economies emerged. Adrian Cadbury made the point: 'We had never been strong enough by ourselves in South East Asia, Central and South America, parts of Africa and the West Indies.' Schweppes, represented for instance in Venezuela, had been pondering a sales effort in South America for some years, and with Cadbury's backing decided to take the plunge. Cadbury could help Schweppes with its food side. 'We had over-invested in foods,' said Lord Watkinson, who pruned the Hartley and Chivers acquisitions. As far back as 1967, Watkinson had asked the accountants, Cooper Brothers, to make suggestions for the company's development as an international organization in the 'seventies. Cooper's report urged that Schweppes should broaden its home base before enlarging its overseas interests; this thinking lay behind the acquisition of Typhoo.

It was on the basis of the Cooper Brothers' study that Lord Watkinson, as chairman of Schweppes, made a personal and informal approach to Adrian Cadbury, the chief executive of British Cocoa. There followed a number of detailed meetings between the main board directors of both companies, in which the merger plan was examined in further detail. There was no product overlap between the two groups and, therefore, none of the problems of merging brand leaders in the same product field. The aims considered by Lord Watkinson and Adrian Cadbury were highlighted by a marketing conference in London in November 1968, when each of them was struck by the similarity of the other's approach. This spurred on the informal talks which also brought out further points of similarity – notably that both companies had recently retained consultants and in each case this had led to the conversion of a rather loose federal grouping into a market-orientated structure. Schweppes' overseas profits had doubled in the previous four years and were 25 per cent up in 1968 at £2·5 million. Cadbury's group sales had increased from £115 million in 1965 to around £150 million in 1968, and, of that total, 37 per cent were overseas sales. The ensuing discussions lasted six weeks in London and Birmingham and covered organization, finance, marketing, production, overseas operations, and purchasing.

The two boards identified six major areas for possible co-operation:

(a) To build up a worldwide organization with resources for breaking into new markets;
(b) To expand research and development in new products;
(c) To develop joint expansion in the British catering and vending markets;
(d) To develop jointly the leaf and instant tea market;
(e) To share production and distribution facilities;
(f) To realize economies of scale in buying, training, administration, and advertising.

The merger discussions were particularly detailed: Cadbury-Schweppes had the great advantage, over many other mergers, of a thorough-going assessment before the merger itself took place. The terms of the merger gave rise to some negotiation. At the annual meeting of Schweppes called to endorse the deal, Lord Watkinson revealed that when the merger had been first planned, Schweppes and its advisers had fixed a maximum price for the offer which had been rejected by the Cadbury board. The talks had then been called off, until new negotiations resulted in an offer acceptable to both boards.

Stock Exchange Rumours

By the beginning of 1969, the merger had been almost wholly agreed.

Towards the end of January, a burst of stock exchange rumours led to heavy trading in Cadbury shares. Following the General Foods-Rowntree affair, there had been rumours that Beecham might bid for Schweppes, or that Cadbury might support a bid from one of the big US or European food groups. This time, the rumours were at least partly justified, though there was some undue optimism about Cadbury's share price. News of the negotiations between Cadbury and Schweppes was revealed on 28 January, and the terms of the merger were announced the following day. The mechanics of the deal involved a share offer by Schweppes for Cadbury, the effect of which was to divide the ordinary share capital of the new group between the ordinary shareholders of the two companies in almost exactly equal proportions. Kleinwort Benson, the traditional advisers to Schweppes, sent out the offer, while Cadbury's support was underpinned by its financial advisers, Samuel Montagu, and City accountants, Binder Hamlyn.

After the merger the Cadbury-Fry families and trusts became the major holders in the new group, controlling about 25 per cent of the equity. The merger company ranked eighth in the world league table, with a turnover of £250 million. Apart from Nestlé, which is three times larger, Cadbury-Schweppes ranked as the only non-US organization among the world's top dozen food companies. For some time, there were doubts about whether the Board of Trade would refer the Cadbury-Schweppes merger to the Monopolies Commission. There was little overlap between the two groups, except to a limited degree in food, while existing co-operation was limited to one minor project between Schweppes' drink side and Pascall over drink and sweet trollies on garage forecourts. On 30 January 1969, Lord Watkinson wrote to members of the Schweppes executive committee: 'Unfortunately we now face another hazard, namely the distinct possibility that the Board of Trade may refer this merger to the Monopolies Commission and thus impose a further delay of possibly three or four months.' But in that same memorandum Lord Watkinson stressed the two key factors, which probably induced the Board of Trade in the event not to refer the merger proposal, that there was 'no product overlap' and that both he and Adrian Cadbury had given 'firm assurances that the identity of the two companies will be maintained – possibly for some considerable time'.

The following month, Cadbury and Schweppes received official consent to go ahead, and the two boards wasted little time in pushing ahead with the merger.

In April 1969, a new division was announced within the food group to draw together both concerns' activities in the catering industry, and to help supply the fast growing food vending-machine business. In June, a far reaching move created a branded foods division to include both Cadbury's and Schweppes food production and marketing. This division, a £25 million a year business, was based at Bournville and headed by Bob

Wadsworth, the former Cadbury man who sat on the main Cadbury-Schweppes board.

Common Identity

On 31 July, Lord Watkinson made an important statement to the Bournville works council meeting: 'I would say that we want to maintain, and improve wherever possible, this feeling of a common identity and a common purpose.' He pointed to one of the merger group's major problems: 'An immense number of different practices across the company and different methods of reward, profit sharing, bonus systems, merit ratings, productivity agreements, to mention only a few.' Lord Watkinson made clear that the current negotiation and joint consultation procedures would change very little 'for some time to come', though Frank Hamer, the newly appointed director of personnel for the merger company, began a detailed study of Cadbury-Schweppes' pay structures, consultation, and communications.

Not long after Lord Watkinson's speech, another post-merger reshuffle was completed with the merging of the overseas division of Schweppes and Cadbury to form Cadbury-Schweppes Overseas. This new group was given a new board of management under Basil Collins, a main board director.

Group results for the first half of the year 1969, published at the beginning of October, provided the first public test of the merger. Against the forecast of rather better than £20 million, which was contained in the formal merger document issued in March, the group showed profits of some £8 million for the January to June period.

Turnover, comparing half-year 1968 with half-year 1969 had risen by rather more than £11 million and trading profits by some £750 000, from £9·44 million to £10·20 million. But this extra trading income was almost wholly off-set by higher interest payments and loan stock interest. Lord Watkinson stressed that these figures 'do not take us anything like half way to our profit target for 1969' partly because of the seasonal nature of the business which for Schweppes, in particular, meant that the Christmas period was always the more profitable. Lord Watkinson explained that it would not be possible during 1969 to reduce high rate bank borrowing, but told shareholders and employees that, subject to any upsets in the Christmas trade, 'we believe we shall achieve over the full year the profits forecast for the time of the merger'.

In his Christmas message Lord Watkinson could feel reasonably justified in saying: 'We have made a good start in welding all our operations together.' To the outside world, the shape of the new group emerged just after the new year, with the formation of five subsidiary companies to set the legal structure for the five major marketing groups. The subsidiaries were Cadbury, Schweppes, Cadbury-Schweppes Overseas, Typhoo, and Cadbury-Schweppes Foods. Responsible to the chairman, Lord Watkinson, and to the

69

deputy chairman, Adrian Cadbury, were the five groups: confectionery under David Borland, drinks under Bob Newcomb, overseas under Basil Collins, tea and coffee under John Tustain, and food under Bob Wadsworth.

That Christmas, one of Cadbury-Schweppes' principal executives, the joint managing director, James Barker, was going through a period of great indecision. He had been offered the chairmanship of the Unigate milk and foods group. Barker decided to accept – a loss for Cadbury-Schweppes but a move which paved the way for a major simplification of the top board structure. The City tends to be sceptical of an organization involving joint managing directors. Barker's resignation meant that Adrian Cadbury could take over as sole managing director as well as deputy chairman. In this way Lord Watkinson, then sixty, and Adrian Cadbury, then forty-one, could work closely together to carry through the post-merger reshaping. The announcement of Barker's resignation was made on 13 January. As well as the appointment of Adrian Cadbury, Basil Collins was appointed chief executive of overseas operations. Two new men, were recruited to the board. Bob Newcomb as chairman of the drinks group and James Forbes, deputy finance director and secretary, who with Adrian Cadbury played a crucial role in preparing financial data for management in the post-merger assessments. James Barker strongly denied the obvious inference that the merger played any part in his joining Unigate. He had been in the soft drinks business all his working life, having started in Roses, the lime juice manufacturers which were taken over by Schweppes back in 1957.

The resignation of James Barker was the most outstanding, but not the only loss to follow the merger. In July, Dennis Curtis, the Schweppes director in charge of group market planning, left to head a new consultancy service for Peat Marwick, the City accountants. An earlier departure, in October 1969, was that of Hugh Miles, marketing director of the confectionery division, who left to take up a similar job with Italy's largest chocolate manufacturer, Ferrero. Miles' departure was reportedly over dissatisfaction on the alternative of improving profits either by cutting the development budget or reducing advertising. Miles had spent all his working life, twenty-two years, with Cadbury and had taken over as marketing director of the confectionery division after the McKinsey inspired reorganization.

James Barker remained at Cadbury-Schweppes until the end of February. In order not to blur the new lines of responsibility which the board reasonably felt should operate straightaway, he agreed to concentrate on relationships with the Ministry of Agriculture, customer relationships, the food budget for 1970, and the restructuring of the food group.

Forecasts Missed

But it was beginning to become clear that the 1969 profit forecasts, made at the time of the original merger, were not going to be met. In his London

Newsletter of November, Lord Watkinson, in pointing out that initial merger progress had been well received in the City, stressed that after six months' experience the merger 'still looks as sound as it looked to Adrian Cadbury and myself before we brought it about'. Writing an appraisal for the directors of Cadbury-Schweppes, Lord Watkinson said bluntly: 'We shall have had a bad year in 1969 made worse by the coping with cocoa price fluctuation.' He explained that the first budgetary exercise held at the end of 1969 had produced a trading profit of only £20 million. This exercise was processed through the main board's finance committee (of which Lord Watkinson himself was chairman) which produced an additional profit improvement target through a combination of savings and increased sales. That target, if achieved, would have produced an extra £2 million trading profit. The board agreed on the two lines of attack: improving the marketing and selling effort and reducing overheads. On the latter, Lord Watkinson was explicit: 'So far as Cadbury and Schweppes overheads are concerned, one plus one has got to equal much less than two, otherwise there is little or no justification for the merger.' The achieving of trading profit targets rested specifically with the deputy chairman and the chairmen of each of the five product groups. As the immediate emphasis lay on overheads, Lord Watkinson looked for a £500 000 saving through reductions master-minded by Adrian Cadbury, assisted by John Tustain, James Forbes, Jack Mudge, Peter Gregory, and Keith Collyer.

But problems were beginning to emerge for the new group. One, unexpectedly, was industrial unrest. In November 1969 a record of fifty years' peaceful co-operation at Bournville was ended. For the first time since 1906, there was talk among the 5000 or so workers of a full scale strike, though union officials stressed: 'This is nothing to do with the merger of Cadbury and Schweppes.' In the event, the company's proposals for the first major reshuffle for over thirty years were initially thrown out by the production workers. At the same time, Cadbury executives saw 400 men on a night shift walk out over a manning dispute – a rare move at Bournville. One of the underlying problems facing Cadbury was that earnings did not compare well with those paid at the nearby car plants in Birmingham and Coventry.

Shortfall Explained

By early 1970, Lord Watkinson and his colleagues realized that the group would not achieve its merger target for profits: the out-turn, as shown in the annual accounts published in May, was £18·1 million, ignoring minority interests, against the merger forecast of not less than £20 million. Lord Watkinson explained to shareholders the causes of the shortfall: confectionery sales were below budget, Christmas trade was somewhat disappointing on the drinks side, tea consumption in Britain had declined though the overseas side had improved. He pointed out that 1970 would be the first complete year of operation for the group when the industrial logic of the merger should begin to show results. Behind Lord Watkinson's analysis lay an unusual and comprehensive self-examination carried out at meetings in London by the fifty or so top executives of Cadbury-Schweppes during the early weeks of 1970.

The picture which emerged presents an intriguing portrait of a group poised for the development of a large, and clearly logical merger which had run into short term problems. The starting point of the analysis was to set out the structure of the group in early 1970, roughly a year after the merger had been legally completed.

Out of the total Cadbury-Schweppes labour force of more than 40 000, about 12 700 worked overseas. At home some 12 500 were employed in confectionery, just over 10 800 in food, some 4750 in drinks, and just under 800 in tea. But the profitability of these various divisions varied considerably: tea, small and highly capitalized, showed the unusually high figure of £4700 profit per employee; drinks produced £836, confectionery £380, but food as little as £220. This formed the first basis for the view that any far reaching profit improvement by Cadbury-Schweppes would probably include some reshaping of the two companies' food side in order to improve average profitability.

On capital, Cadbury-Schweppes employed some £190 million of gross assets, made up of roughly £120 million fixed assets and some £70 million working capital. Of the £190 million, just over £60 million was employed overseas. At home, the largest single division but, remember, yielding the lowest profit per employee, was food, with just over £57 million, confectionery came a close second with some £53 million, drinks next with £22 million, while tea had rather less than £10 million. By the standard of trading profit on capital employed, the food side showed more normal figures, though both food and confectionery showed below average earnings for 1969–70. For Cadbury-Schweppes as a whole, earnings on capital were some 13 per cent, reflecting a 16 per cent average yield overseas and one of 12 per cent in Britain. Among the four major home divisions, tea showed the unusually high ratio of no less than 34 per cent; drinks came second with 17 per cent, whereas confectionery and food (together employing more than half the group assets) earned no more than 6 per cent each. Cadbury-Schweppes' short term problems were increased by its being highly geared in terms of trading profit towards gross income. The group was spending about £20 million a year on advertising and marketing, plus another £10·5 million a year on distribution. Other overheads absorbed no less than £18 million – a major target for future rationalization.

The 1970 plan, which was the initial basis for the recovery initiated by Lord Watkinson and Adrian Cadbury, was that the overseas side should produce 40 per cent of the profits, while contributing 38 per cent of the sales, 35 per cent of the capital employed, and 30 per cent of the total labour force.

At home, the group had been affected by slow economic growth and a legacy of overheads on the production side.

Cadbury-Schweppes had suffered from the squeeze on credit which formed the basis of economic policy from 1968 to 1970. The principal effect on the group was to slow down the capital spending programme. By the spring of 1970, about £4·5 million of capital spending was firmly committed, or had been held over from the previous year. This left the board with the power to review more than £4 million worth of schemes. One of its difficulties was that only about one-third of Cadbury-Schweppes' projected capital spending represented large projects, the great bulk went on a host of small items such as replacing trucks, renewing equipment, and so on. It was estimated that no less than £5·6 million was scheduled for schemes that could not be classified as major projects. But of the projects that did loom large, easily the biggest, involving just over £1·1 million, was the expansion of Smash Instant Potato, which had been one of Cadbury's great successes. One other financing problem was the strongly seasonal element of group business which could add between £4 million and £5 million to any given stock figure. While Cadbury-Schweppes had bank borrowing limits of between £30 million and £35 million, a reduction of average stock levels would clearly have eased the financing burden. The overriding aim was to improve the earnings per employee, above all in food. For the City, it was necessary to improve the price-earnings valuation of Cadbury-Schweppes, whose share rating had suffered both from the general stock market setback, by realization of the damage done by the high cocoa prices in 1969, and by some wholly unfounded rumours of dissension between the two sets of Cadbury and Schweppes executives.

As for other consumer-oriented groups, further uncertainties were posed by decimalization in February 1971, which in effect involved a standstill on prices from November 1970 until decimalization day. This meant a carefully planned prices policy for the first half of 1971 and a realization that during the 'price freeze' promotion would necessarily be limited. The great danger for a group like Cadbury-Schweppes was that the distributors, particularly supermarkets, would use a period of this sort to try to exercise greater control over their suppliers.

One Year After

Confectionery

In confectionery, the two great lessons of 1969 were the need to improve the group's buying of cocoa, Cadbury is the largest single buyer in Britain, and the need to improve budgetary supervision, excesses over budget in 1969 came to light too late for effective control. Cadbury suffered from the rise of cocoa prices which took place between 1967 and 1969. By October 1969, for example, the price had reached £425 against £325 a year before and £245 two years before. Profits were reduced as the compensatory increase in selling prices necessarily lagged behind rising material costs. The other critical financial feature of the confectionery side was that it was highly geared: overheads were relatively large. Just how large is shown by a 3 per cent shortfall in sales which produced an adverse profit experience of no less than £600000. A 5 per cent shortfall, of the sort which hit the group during the exceptional period of 1969, brought a profit setback of more than £1 million. Over the long term, it must be an aim of policy to reduce overheads, especially at Bournville.

The other confectionery marketing lessons absorbed in 1969 were the dangers of copying competitors. Probably Cadbury's most obvious imitation was the launch of Aztec to compete with the Mars Bar. Aztec proved less than a great success; and Bar 6, launched on a similar basis, lost some of its earlier impetus.

The major medium and long term problem for Cadbury-Schweppes confectionery group must be to restyle and rejuvenate the presentation of chocolates. Not only do the bulk of Cadbury's brands date back to the 'thirties, but the whole fashion and style of chocolate boxes are themselves old fashioned. Cadbury's market research suggests that a growing and dangerously large number of chocolate boxes are bought as specific presents rather than normal impulse purchases of chocolates. To meet this, a special production team was set up to reshape the packaging of chocolates. One of the immediate proposals was to merge the sales forces of Cadbury and Fry, a momentous move for Fry, which had been extremely proud of its independent tradition.

A structural difficulty for Cadbury-Schweppes is the lack of balance between chocolate and sugar confectionery. Cadbury estimated that it held about 35 per cent of the chocolate confectionery market but only about 4 per cent of the sugar confectionery market. (Its sugar confectionery interests were represented by Pascall and Murray, bought from Beechams for £1·75 million in 1964.) By contrast, Rowntree-Mackintosh, Cadbury's major competitor, has a much closer balance of chocolate and sugar confectionery, with a 30 per cent and 12 per cent market share respectively.

Drinks

Cadbury-Schweppes gained considerable benefits from a reshaping of discounts to the drinks trade. Against this, the drink divisions suffered from the ban on cyclamates from January 1970 which cost the group some £200000 in drinks that had to be disposed of. Schweppes' drinks business splits neatly between groceries on the one hand and the licensed and catering trades on the other. Schweppes' view was that development would come through new packaging rather than new products, though the group has an impressive record as innovators, notably the one trip no-deposit bottle.

Based on the view that it would find it difficult to enlarge its share of the licensed trade, Schweppes set about developing complementary areas. One that impressed it was Babycham, which had been so skilfully developed by Showerings. To match this low-alcohol drink, Schweppes launched Vin Rosa, which was test marketed in the London area. It also pondered a carbonated cream drink to take it into the pop market.

Food

Earning adequate profits from Cadbury-Schweppes large food side probably represented one of the major long term problems of the merger. Executives felt that the merger had put together a heterogeneous collection of foods with varying profit margins and different marketing methods. Among the problems of 1969–70 were biscuits, where the group suffered both from a contracting market and from rising cocoa prices. Another problem area was tea, while the Cadbury side had had some difficulties with the launch of Fine Brew Tea; Schweppes' Typhoo side, by contrast, had abstained from moving into instant tea. The one great consolation for Cadbury-Schweppes was Smash, with more than 50 per cent of the market and a turnover of £5 million plus a year. The lessons from 1969 were clear: for Cadbury, sales were on target, but costs were out of control; for Schweppes, sales were out of budget, though costs were on target.

Tea and Coffee

The tea and coffee division, which covers both Typhoo and Kenco, which Schweppes bought from Trust Houses, is a relatively selfcontained unit. Its great long term problem is that the tea market is declining. In the ten years from 1958, according to official statistics, consumption in Britain fell by some 50 million pounds, or just over one pound each year per head of population. Typhoo has, therefore, kept up a high level of spending on advertising. It found that a price promotion in alliance with the supermarkets did not prove successful. During 1969, profits from tea were improved both by the trend of tea prices and by some skilful buying. Typhoo had gained, along with others, from the growth of the tea bag market, where sales had doubled in 1969 and were expected to double in 1970, but this did not produce the heavy volume of 'normal' tea sales. Typhoo executives had pondered a second brand, but it was far from clear whether this should be above or below Typhoo's market position. Typhoo admitted to being slow in the own-brand market which it had not developed before the Schweppes takeover; this was frankly conceded to have been a mistake.

So much for the particular sections of the Cadbury-Schweppes business. A great deal of discussion also centred on the lines of broad strategy. One of the prime questions was whether the group could use elsewhere the successful sales methods such as telephone selling services employed in drinks. Adrian

Cadbury stressed the need to combine services within divisions in order to reduce central overheads. He felt that one of the major areas for economy lay in the sales accounting forces used by all divisions, but which were not co-ordinated. This was taken a step further by Lord Watkinson, who believed that one division should accept an idea which had been successful in another, unless the division where it was to be applied could convince the executive committee that the idea would not succeed, a simple refusal would not be enough.

Everyone agreed that there should be no more use of outside consultants; both groups had employed McKinsey, and Schweppes had also employed Urwick Orr and Arthur D. Little. One of the basic problems posed by the market-oriented structure favoured by these consultants was that it increased the need for strong control at the centre; powerful market-oriented divisions could easily turn into independent empires.

One of the keys to Cadbury-Schweppes development must lie in profit improvement – one of the favourite terms employed by consultants. Monthly returns quickly became standard throughout the group, based on the four-weekly returns which had originated in Schweppes' drinks side because of the seasonal nature of the business. But there were some differences over the use of the term 'profit improvement', because many Cadbury-Schweppes executives felt that productivity or earnings improvement would be more suitable terms especially for discussion with trade unions. They admired the profit improvement carried out by Procter and Gamble between 1951 and 1967. This showed one of the great merits of a profit-improvement campaign, that it produces a series of take-off points. In other words, that a steady programme of profit improvement can induce acceleration of profit growth at high levels.

Policy Differences

A year after the merger, policies differed considerably. This is, after all, not hard to understand: the Schweppes food side had gone through no less than six mergers. The two businesses are also, as became clear, subject to different pressures: drink is a highly seasonal business, confectionery much less so, and food hardly at all. One of the toughest questions posed by the Cadbury-Schweppes executives, which will be of crucial importance for group development over the next few years, centres on the optimum size of factories. On the drinks side, no less than fifteen factories were in operation; a strict theoretical optimum could well be no more than four, but it looks as though changes over the next five years will still leave the group with about eight drinks plants. The two constraining factors from reaching the optimum are the greater management demands posed by large units and the vulnerability of large units to industrial action.

Rationalization, which is a specific responsibility of the main board under

76

Adrian Cadbury, could well serve as a focus for many aspects of Cadbury-Schweppes policy. In confectionery, the programme seems now to be agreed, leaving this side of the business with two large factories, probably two smaller ones, and half a dozen depots. The limited degree of rationalization carried out in the merger's first year worked well.

Shortly after the merger, the board decided to close the Pascall factory at Mitcham, which employed some 1200 people. This site had a relatively high value and the transaction showed a discounted cash flow return of more than 40 per cent. Apart from the site, the closing produced an estimated saving of more than £300000 a year, and released capital of more than £750000. All this was achieved for an outlay of less than £500000 and an estimated cash outflow of £800000, which allowed for full payment for redundancies and for the loss of efficiency while production was being run down and transferred to the Fry factory.

On the tea side, an investigation was also made as to whether it would be sensible to transfer the Typhoo factory to Bournville. It was finally decided that there was no case for doing so, partly because the Typhoo site was less valuable than expected. Another reason was that at Typhoo the factory costs of production represented a small proportion of the total.

Where does this leave the Cadbury-Schweppes group? Over the long term, the merger of two consumer-oriented, complementary businesses must make sense, though over the short term the prime preoccupation will be to meet the profit forecasts made at the time of the merger in early 1969. The results for 1970 are a pointer, but the full scope of the new strategy can hardly emerge before the middle of the decade.

Overseas trade, where the group should be earning 50 per cent of its trading profits in a few years' time, presents perhaps the fewest problems. Cadbury-Schweppes overseas side contains a diversity of interests, ranging from wholly owned subsidiaries (North America), to locally quoted subsidiaries (South Africa and Australia), associate companies (France and Belgium), and franchise operations (Spain). Both companies' overseas interests were known to be well suited for combining and, by the end of the first year after the merger, plans for integration in Australia, North America, and South Africa were practically complete. Cadbury-Schweppes major problem in overseas development remains the mandatory and 'voluntary' restraints imposed by the Treasury on investment overseas. These make it difficult to finance overseas operations direct from Britain, and thus hamper sensible long run expansion.

At home, much of the merger group's success will depend on the policy adopted towards the two big divisions, confectionery and above all foods. The figures already quoted, of relative productivity by division, underline that an improvement in these two units is essential to successful progress. Another illustration of the same problem is that at the time of the merger

Schweppes was producing £10 million a year of profits from £30 million of capital, compared with Cadbury's similar profit from £80 million of capital. Schweppes' drinks side, the base of its business, is well organized with tight financial control and good marketing. Tea, too, is efficiently organized (as the relative productivity figures show), though the board will have to attend to future marketing and produce development. All four divisions of Cadbury-Schweppes are now run on a market-oriented basis with decentralized management.

Food Problems

In food, both groups have problems. Lord Watkinson criticized Schweppes' investment in food when he became managing director six years before the merger. For Cadbury and Schweppes together, the problem lies in reshaping a division which makes no less than 200 individual lines ranging from instant potato and chocolate biscuits to jams and jellies. A number of these 200 items, which seem far too many for a sector with total annual sales of £50 million or so, seem likely to disappear, with little cost to sales and useful benefits to profits. The next few years will show Cadbury-Schweppes skill at carrying through this reshaping.

In confectionery, the problem is essentially one of production, though long term marketing is also important. There is a view in the trade that Cadbury should use its strong market position for more aggressive price leadership. But a prime aim must be to reduce overheads at Bournville, where Cadbury had begun to make substantial progress even before the merger. The post-merger labour disputes were not an auspicious sign, but Bournville's old established and elaborate production systems stood in need of overhaul.

Lord Watkinson and Adrian Cadbury had always intended to complete the major rationalization programme during 1970. In the summer of that year, this seemed unlikely to be achieved, but a poor reception of Cadbury-Schweppes interim results, which was somewhat unfair as there was no comparison of like with like for the half-year between 1969 and 1970, convinced both Watkinson and Cadbury that this was the time to put through the remaining measures. These measures included getting rid of most of the Moreton plant and carrying out fundamental rationalization at Bournville involving management as well as clerical staff. A major psychological step at Bournville was the decision to close the Franklin office block, a large new modern building which represented the headquarters of the food group. These measures represented the completion of Cadbury-Schweppes major measures of rationalization by 1970, as the board had originally planned.

A critical factor in the rationalization programme was the setting up of an Operations Profitability Committee whose first action was to cut the salaries of executive main board directors by 10 per cent. This demonstrated the

78

seriousness with which the entire top management at Cadbury-Schweppes faced rationalization, and made the task itself much easier. At Bournville, much of the work fell on Adrian Cadbury, an operation which for him was particularly difficult.

In early October 1970, Watkinson had set out the purposes of the Operations Profitability Committee: 'To take difficult decisions which must result in cuts in functions and in employment right across the scale from management to the shop floor.' The main board was, therefore, asked to accept a 10 per cent cut in salary for six months at least and directors were asked to submit to further discipline:

(a) No director to take more than four weeks holiday during the following twelve months;

(b) No director to have the authority to make overseas visits unless these were first cleared with the chairman of the overseas group;

(c) Major reductions were sought in 'peripheral expenditure'.

Travelling expenditure, Watkinson wrote, was far too high, and even directors' eating came under scrutiny: 'We must not subsidise the meals in directors' dining rooms . . .' The committee met weekly and its decisions were implemented by Adrian Cadbury.

Not much of this became apparent to the public, for whom the mid year results, published in late September, provided the main guide. These covered twenty-four weeks to 20 June 1970, against the 1969 data for the Cadbury group and Typhoo which covered a full six months. Ignoring the differences in comparability, which many shareholders and the public seemed to do, the picture was of a rise in turnover to £127 million, but of group trading profits of £9·06 million against £10·12 million, and a sharper fall in before tax profits which emerged at £7·17 million against £8·85 million. Retained profits declined to £1 million compared with £1·65 million.

Lord Watkinson explained that all home groups were facing major rises in costs and added: 'Coinciding with financial re-organisation, these rises have had a severe effect on the profits of the foods group, and to a lesser extent on confectionery.' He also explained in the statement that the integration of Cadbury's and Schweppes' food operations had imposed 'further heavy stresses' on the financial control system, but a complete reorganization of financial control and accounting systems in confectionery and foods was being carried out. Lord Watkinson added that the overseas group had been reorganized and its headquarters located at Marble Arch; heavy forward commitments for cocoa, which had distorted profit figures, were also reduced to manageable proportions, and purchasing methods had been changed. A 'fundamental' reorganization of the total computer operation had been found necessary, while the sale of the McColl retailing interests improved cash flow and enabled the group to concentrate on its main purpose of manufacturing and distributing food, drink, and confectionery products.

D

Rationalization Speeded

Referring to foods and confectionery, Lord Watkinson also added: 'It is likely that both groups will face some shortfall in the budgeted profits for the year.' He continued: 'Under these circumstances, the task of securing an improvement over last year's profits will be a very difficult one.' Lord Watkinson explained the strategy behind his thinking in a private newsletter sent out in mid November: 'It may be that the country, and possibly the government, underestimated the difficulties of achieving the sharp change of course which the government proposes that the nation should take.' Watkinson drew the moral from the government's attitude towards taxation and industrial relations: 'We have picked the right time to bring rationalisation through to its final initial phase.' Watkinson conceded that the interim results were 'very disappointing' and these results led both Watkinson and Cadbury to produce proposals to speed up plans for rationalization. Watkinson set out the rationale of the Operations Profitability Committee. This met under his chairmanship, along with Adrian Cadbury as managing director, Basil Collins, David Borland, James Forbes, and Douglas Simmons as secretary. The committee also included two special executives, Peter Gregory and Jack Mudge, who acted on behalf of the committee, and therefore, for the board as a whole.

In late November, a public statement by Cadbury-Schweppes set out the broad lines of rationalization. Production at Moreton was cut back to a limited number of product lines and the rest of the factory leased. The final phase of the 1970 programme covered primarily the employees at Bournville, where the labour force was reduced to about 250 against a total labour force of about 8750. Of those asked to leave, Cadbury-Schweppes explained that 85 would be management staff, 80 non-management regular employees, and the remainder 85 seasonal employees who did not expect to work for more than a few weeks or months. Some 450 jobs were expected to become surplus, 125 management and 320 non-management. Of this total, about 200 were expected to be covered by natural labour turnover, retirements, and transfers. This completed, the statement continued, the major portion of the rationalization plan which had been continuing since March 1969.

Further efficiency and cost-reducing measures were planned for 1971, but for 1970 it was stated that the rationalization measures 'have been completed to plan and have achieved the cost-saving target set by the board'. The statement conceded that the redundancies at Bournville could pose particular problems: 'It would be difficult to offer alternative employment to certain specialists and managers, whose particular skills and opportunities within Cadbury-Schweppes are limited.' Staff were offered assistance through the DEP's executive register for managers, and the New Opportunities Association, of which Cadbury-Schweppes was a founder member. Contacts were also made with other employers in the Birmingham area.

80

Cadbury-Schweppes looks one of the most natural of mergers. In addition to its basic industrial logic, the group has as chairman, Lord Watkinson, who pulled Schweppes out of its diversification difficulties, and as deputy chairman, Adrian Cadbury, who ranks as one of the outstanding figures in younger British management. Cadbury-Schweppes rates high for the extent of planning and discussion that goes on among all senior executives. Cadbury-Schweppes faces real problems; but it has a powerful management team and it has carried through the necessary analysis. On the basis of no more than moderate optimism for the growth of the economy as a whole, the merger should prove a great success.

EMI : A Study in Expansion

In late 1954, a Lancashire milling engineer called Joseph Lockwood became chairman of Electric and Musical Industries, now EMI Ltd. He had been called in partly at the instigation of City interests, who had helped to float EMI before the Second World War, to carry out a drastic rescue operation; and he spent his first Friday as chairman in the City of London raising £1 million from EMI's bankers in order to pay the wages.

Formed in 1931 to place a major part of the world's gramophone record production under one management, EMI was in serious difficulty. It was valued on the London Stock Exchange at only £3 million – barely one-third of the assets which had been put together by Alfred Clark and Louis Sterling a quarter of a century before. EMI had been slow to adopt the 33 and 45 rpm microgroove records which had been introduced in the US during the late 'forties; the domestic appliance side along with radios, television, and record players, was losing £750 000 a year; the potentially valuable electronics business which had grown fast during the Second World War, was in need of reorganization.

Lockwood's immediate problem was that EMI's business had been organized along functional lines. Thus EMI studios made and sold records which were manufactured by EMI factories and distributed by EMI sales and service. By this principle, each company was allowed to buy or sell outside the group if that appeared more profitable, with the result that a manufacturing company could produce a product for an outside concern to market, while the corresponding EMI selling company was buying in the product from an outside manufacturer.

Lockwood's immediate response was to reshape EMI along product lines. During 1955 and 1956, he scrapped the functional divisions in favour of broad product sectors. He also decided that EMI should concentrate on two major sectors: gramophone records and military and commercial electronic capital equipment. This meant taking EMI first out of radio and television and, much later, out of domestic appliances. He pulled EMI out of radio and television by forming the British Radio Corporation with Sir Jules Thorn's Thorn Electric. EMI continued to make and sell radios and television sets in overseas markets but, in Britain, Thorn made all sets under its own mark, Ferguson, and under the HMV and Marconiphone trademarks owned by EMI.

The deal with Thorn released valuable manufacturing assets at EMI's Hayes headquarters. Further facilities were released in 1960 when EMI bought control of Morphy-Richards. This takeover produced an unusual tussle, in which the Morphy-Richards board at first resisted the bid. Confronted by EMI's generous bid terms, it finally left shareholders to decide for themselves. EMI won by bidding high and by its acquisition of shares from Donal Morphy, one of the original founders of the firm who had decided to sell out. Morphy-Richards proved an expensive acquisition; sales of consumer durables were soon to suffer from the series of stop-go measures introduced by successive Conservative and Labour Chancellors, while it became clear that Morphy-Richards' production facilities, at St Mary Cray in Kent, could not easily be adapted to a wider range of goods. In 1966, when all British manufacturers of electrical consumer goods were suffering from overcapacity, EMI merged Morphy-Richards with AEI's consumer durable interests to form British Domestic Appliances which, in turn, later joined forces with GEC and English Electric.

Despite the problems which he faced on joining EMI, Joseph Lockwood and his colleagues made an important decision, namely the purchase of Capitol Records of Los Angeles. This took place only a few months after Lockwood joined EMI. After the Second World War, the distribution of EMI records in the US was handled through an agreement between EMI itself, Radio Corporation of America, and Columbia. This agreement was threatened by anti-trust action in the US, so EMI looked for a distribution company of which it could buy control. EMI paid £3 million for Capitol, which has proved an outstandingly successful investment: in early 1970, the 72 per cent interest in Capitol (which in 1968 had taken over Audio Devices in a share deal) was worth over £20 million.

Lockwood's reshaping of EMI worked wonders for sales and profits from the mid 'fifties onwards. More records sold as living standards rose. It was first through records, and later through clothes and fashion, that teenagers established their importance as a market. Long term, one of Lockwood's most important aims was to build up the overseas interests of EMI, which were to give the group such a strong position in the late 'sixties. Local policies were adapted to group developments. EMI was careful to adapt its trading policies to changing conditions in the new nations of Africa, and it extended its market penetration through new subsidiaries, licencees, and distributors.

The story of these years is best told in the financial data of the decade from 1959. Sales throughout the world grew from just under £70 million to rather more than £120 million; capital employed grew from £20 million to £80 million; and before tax profits from £5 million to more than £11 million.

Beatles Turnover

Probably EMI's best known coup in these years was its contract with that young team who, so the story goes, had been turned down by one of EMI's rivals. The Beatles, who began to show up in EMI statistics during 1963, grossed more than £6 million for themselves and the group during their first year, and probably contributed about £5 million to £6 million annually after that. In the US, the Beatles represented as much as 10 per cent of EMI's total turnover, under a long term contract which netted the Beatles about 1p on every disc, 4p for every long-playing record, and 6·25 per cent on the retail price for music which they wrote themselves.

EMI's success brought a sharp rise in its stock market rating, while the growth of Capitol (of which EMI held sole control until the Audio takeover) brought in US investors as shareholders. But during the early and mid 'sixties, EMI had to face new problems. The first was the growth of cut-price records – as purchase tax grew steadily higher – and the invasion of the attractive UK market by US and European companies. Over a period, this meant that EMI could no longer maintain the 40 to 50 per cent market share it had held during the late 'fifties, but had to be content with a share nearer 20 to 25 per cent – which still left the group in the leading position in Britain.

The second major change affecting EMI was the decision by a number of leading US industrial groups to move into the leisure industry. Leisure had become a growing business in its own right, attractive to the new generation of conglomerates who set about reviving some of the old established cinema and communications groups which had fallen on hard times. For EMI, this new trend in the US meant stronger competition, and it also brought much closer the prospect of a bid from the US. To a possible US buyer, EMI, valued by London standards, looked an attractive proposition. Even more important, a number of US groups looked enviously at the large overseas network which EMI had built up.

By early 1967, EMI was worth £45 million in stock market values – a long way from the £3 million which Sir Joseph Lockwood had inherited, but still leaving EMI open to a takeover. Capitol, despite a setback in 1963, had become a valuable property, and no less than £13 million of the £45 million capitalization were represented by cash or near-cash assets. It was at this point that EMI first heard that the Grade Organization might be up for sale. Founded just after the Second World War, the Grade Organization represented the show business interests of the Grade brothers, Lew Grade, the founder of ATV, Leslie Grade, and Bernard Delfont. Just before the deal with EMI, the Grade Organization had acquired the Shipman and King cinema chain from the Danziger brothers. EMI's bid for Grade, which was completed in the spring of 1967, cost £7·5 million. The deal carefully extended EMI's interests, helped to add to its total size, and place £3 million plus of EMI shares in firm hands. The Grade acquisition proved the

84

first crucial stage in moving EMI into the film and entertainment business. Only a few months after buying Grade, EMI paid £5 million for the Blackpool Tower, that very British institution in which a large slice of Blackpool entertainment is held. Blackpool Tower Co. brought into EMI, among other things, a zoo, a circus, an aquarium, and a motor vehicle business.

Electronic Expansion

EMI's massive takeover, the bid battle for Associated British Picture Corporation, came in 1968–69. In the intervening years, Joseph Lockwood and John Read, his managing director, carried through a series of smaller bids to develop EMI's electronic interests. After playing a major role, before the Second World War, in the development of television electronics, EMI received a major boost from 1939 to 1945 from the development of radar systems, which led the group into guidance and telemetry. Sir Joseph Lockwood slimmed down the variety of EMI's electronic side, but soon decided that this should be a major growth area. A large part of EMI's electronic business, which grew, according to one informed estimate from about £25 million in 1963 to £35 million in 1968, represented government contracts, but the aim was steadily to enlarge the commercial part (EMI's military electronics included the fusing of missiles, sound systems, and reconnaissance equipment for the Phantom). EMI gained little direct benefit from the expansion of data processing during the 'sixties, as its own computer interests were sold to International Computers in exchange for shares. A wholesale move into computers would have involved a major investment of group capital, and a strategic shift of resources, which the board decided to avoid. One of John Read's aims as managing director had been to improve the growth potential of electronics. An important step was to put EMI into medical electronics by the acquisition of SE Laboratories, a small but highly successful company formed, ten years before the EMI takeover, by Rolf Schild and Peter Epstein and which had established a major position in medical equipment. The attraction for EMI was that it took the group into sophisticated medical hardware. The Ministry of Technology cast a benevolent eye on EMI's plans, partly because the lack of development of such equipment in Britain meant a great deal had to be imported.

Another important expansion move was the bid for Associated Fire Alarms, one of the leading British companies in civilian security and fire-protection systems. EMI's aim was to exploit for civilian use the infra-red and other sensing devices which it had developed originally for military purposes. EMI also made some smaller takeovers, including Nickols Automatics and Precision Electronic, to enlarge its industrial electronics capacity. EMI's principal short term aim was to improve the growth prospects, and raise the profitability of its electronic side, where British earnings were low: hence the far reaching reorganization which was carried through in the summer of 1969. This reshaped the electronics and industrial operations into divisions based on product range and market orientation. The divisions include: tubes and microelectronics; television equipment; radar; weapons; sound products; and computer peripherals. This reshaping, plus some reduction in the proportion of government work – a rising market but a falling proportionate total – was planned to put EMI's electronics and industrial operations on a more profitable basis overall.

But the key takeover by EMI, whose success will have a major effect on group performance over the next few years, resulted from the battle for the Associated British Picture Corporation. EMI had decided to concentrate on electronics and records, the latter proving a profitable but competitive business, the former a solid if rather uninspiring profit base. The Grade takeover which came at a time when EMI might have been vulnerable to a bid, pushed the group along the path of entertainment development. Then along came ABPC.

ABPC was the creation of a Scots lawyer, John Maxwell, who started in the industry as an exhibitor, owning a cinema in Glasgow. He soon realized that to have any bargaining power with distributors, he needed greater booking capacity. He thus began to acquire more cinemas. Having acquired cinemas, he decided that to ensure an adequate supply of films he needed to secure a measure of control over distribution. John Maxwell also shared J. Arthur Rank's view that the British film industry should be free from domination by the big US production and distribution companies.

Maxwell moved to London, where his business expanded fast. He took over Elstree Studios in 1927 and bought out the Pathé brothers, who were well known through Pathé News and Pathé Pictorial. In 1928, Maxwell founded Associated British Cinemas, to unite the forty cinemas which he then owned. Five years later, ABC changed its name to the Associated British Picture Corporation, and the following year merged with British International Pictures, which by then owned a chain of 150 cinemas.

Warners Tie-Up

A tie-up with Warner Brothers of the US came later, though Maxwell had been associated with Warners through National Pathé. It was in 1941 that Warners bought £2 million ordinary shares from Maxwell's widow. This bought Warners a 25 per cent holding in ABPC. In 1945, Warners purchased a further million shares from Mrs Maxwell and her trustees. This raised its holding to 37·5 per cent, and put Warners, along with Mrs Maxwell and her trustees, in a position where they owned more than half the equity of ABPC. Although Warners nominated two directors, the chairman was still put forward by the Maxwell interests, and there were specific undertakings between Warners and ABPC that the British company should 'remain free at all time to rent pictures from such sources as it might think fit'. In 1961, Warners sold a million of its shares in ABPC; that deal brought its holding back to the 25 per cent level at which it remained until the deal with EMI nearly ten years later.

ABPC's postwar record, so far as shareholders were concerned, was less than exciting. It owned the second largest chain of cinemas in Britain, in an industry which went into sharp decline immediately after the early postwar years as television began to spread. The feature of ABPC's position, which was to precipitate the takeover from EMI, was its association with Warner Brothers. Warner Brothers, one of the founder families of the US cinema, normally appointed a director, but played little part in ABPC policy. But profit-conscious corporations moved into the traditional and highly personalized US cinema industry. This was the trend which concerned the EMI board; for Warner Brothers, it brought a bid from Seven Arts, and the new company took a hard look at its holdings in ABPC.

Warner-Seven Arts lost little time in making up its mind about the ABPC shareholding. Warner Brothers merged in the summer of 1967, and the new board faced two possibilities, an outright bid or a sale. An outright bid at prevailing market prices would have cost something in the order of £40 million and, under British Treasury rules, it would have to be made wholly in cash. Moreover, there seemed little logic in Warner investing a large amount of money in acquiring a British film distribution set-up. The alternative was to sell.

Warners was involved in discussions in London and with a number of US companies. Sir Joseph Lockwood heard that Warner Brothers wanted to sell and negotiations began. One problem for EMI was that under the City of London's takeover rules, it would have to assess the merits of making a bid for the entire share capital of ABPC if it bought Warner's 25 per cent interest. A complete bid would represent an investment of £40 million plus which needed financing and necessarily carried important implications for the medium and long term development of the group.

Early in 1968, stock market rumours led to heavy speculation in ABPC shares. And on 31 January, EMI announced that it had agreed to pay £9·5 million or £2·37½ a share for the 25 per cent (4 million out of the total 16 million shares), held by Warner Brothers. Sir Joseph Lockwood also disclosed that EMI was willing to make an offer for the other 12 million shares, representing 75 per cent of the ordinary share capital in ABPC, at the same price.

One immediate complication for a complete bid by EMI was the role of the Independent Television Authority. The Warner Brothers deal also required Bank of England and Board of Trade permission. (The Bank of England because foreign exchange was involved and the Board of Trade because of the cinema interests.) ITA held the crucial power to sanction the transfer of voting interests in commercial television companies. ABPC held a half share in Thames Television, the other half being held by Rediffusion, which, under the current reallocation of licences, had been given the all important contract covering the London area. ITA launched the rather chilly statement that it had: 'Informed EMI and ABPC that its approval to the acquisition of the Warner Brothers-Seven Arts holding carries no implications that a further acquisition of AB Pictures would be approved.' EMI replied specifically that it wished to safeguard the television interests of ABPC, but it was already clear that ITA supervision of ABPC television interests was likely to prove a major obstacle.

EMI went to considerable lengths to reassure the Board of Trade and ITA, especially over the position of the talent agencies which it had inherited with the Grade Organization takeover back in 1967. At the outset of negotiations with ITA, EMI offered to sell these off. As the Board of Trade was concerned about the acquisition of cinema interests (EMI was already involved in a small way in the cinema business through Grade's Shipman and King chain), EMI also gave assurances about film production and distribution. These apparently went down well with the Board of Trade which, however, inserted the crucial proviso that ITA should approve the television arrangements.

ITA Negotiations

The negotiations with ITA at that stage were the turning-point. The EMI team was headed by Sir Joseph Lockwood, the chairman, along with his two key directors, John Read (later the chief executive) and Bernard Delfont. They made three sets of proposals to ITA, all of which involved ABC Television taking a non-voting rather than voting share in Thames Television. Under two of the schemes put forward, the voting control, perhaps between 10 and 25 per cent of ABC Television's total capital, would pass to those who ran the television companies.

EMI's opening proposal to ITA was that Thames Television should be controlled by Rediffusion, the other partner. This was a particularly astute move by EMI, because ITA itself had inserted in the Thames Television contract that:

> In the event of the Authority . . . coming to the conclusion that there had been, or that there were about to be, material changes in the stockholdings of the Corporation which would result in too great a concentration of stock at any one source . . . that ABC Television would be required . . . automatically to exchange with Rediffusion Television shareholders in Thames a number of voting shares, the intention being . . . the control of Thames would pass to Rediffusion Television.

But ITA refused to accept any of EMI's three proposals. It laid down instead that EMI should, if it gained control of ABPC, sell off 75 per cent of the ABC Television equity to the shareholders in ABPC. EMI, on that basis, would be left with 25 per cent of the television company's equity and, therefore, with only 12·5 per cent in Thames Television itself. EMI pondered the ITA suggestion and then with reluctance turned it down flat. For the public, its statement simply ran: 'The required conditions are not in the interests of the shareholders of either company, nor in the best interests of the employees of AB Picture.' EMI's reasoning was twofold: first, Sir Joseph felt that the price that EMI would get for television holdings sold in this way would be too poor to justify going ahead with the bid for the whole of ABPC. Second, both EMI and the ABPC directors themselves were concerned about the position of employees in ABC Television.

ITA were, of course, acting on solid legal ground; the Television Act of 1964 laid down that the Authority could withdraw a contract when ownership of the operating company changed hands. That seemed reasonable enough, but ITA appeared then to take the rather legalistic view that any changes in ownership of the contracting companies should take place only when the contracts came up for renewal (this would have meant 1974). It was particularly hostile – and this proved the final blow for EMI – to changes in control within months of its original allocation of a contract. In other words, ITA was saying, on grounds of principle, that it was not prepared to see a change in the ownership of Thames Television so soon after it had redrawn the contract.

Bid Collapse

The negotiations between EMI and ITA were long drawn out; but by early April, roughly three months after EMI had agreed to buy the Warner Brothers stake, the breakdown point came. Both the Treasury and the Board of Trade had been satisfied by EMI's plans, but ITA proved obdurate, and the bid collapsed. Within a few days of that announcement, EMI received two profitable offers for its 25 per cent interest in ABPC, but it declined to sell.

Sir Joseph, John Read, and Bernard Delfont had become convinced of two things. One was that there was a major future for EMI in the entertainment business, along the lines already set by the US conglomerates. Second, they had come to believe that ABPC could benefit from an aggressive management, and they considered that it had failed to develop its chances, above all in cinema production, during the postwar years.

ABPC agreed to keep talking and it was accepted that John Read and Bernard Delfont should join the board; in the same way, one of the ABPC directors was to join the board of EMI. The outlines of EMI's thinking became clear in the summer. In early July, it finally agreed to sell off part of the agency side of the Grade Organization to two leading West End names, Robin Fox and Laurence Evans. EMI also indicated that the rest of the agency side would probably be disposed of within the following few months. This deal, which was completed only a few weeks before Thames

89

Television started to broadcast, was intended as a gesture of goodwill towards ITA.

While relations between the two companies were initially cordial, EMI had also come to appreciate that ABPC was unlikely to welcome a bid. Sir Philip Warter and Robert Clark, it was suggested, had not welcomed EMI's third proposal to ITA – to move control of Thames Television to Rediffusion. Sir Philip himself proposed John Read and Bernard Delfont to the ABPC board, though this took an unusually long time to achieve, and seems to have led to a deterioration in relations. It was not until early September that Read and Delfont were put forward by the ABPC chairman: 'They will make a useful addition to the board. I am proposing them myself.' Back in April, Sir Philip had agreed to become the ABPC director on the EMI board, but later had second thoughts. 'They did not ask me to go, and I thought for the moment, with ITA, it was better not.'

EMI was not prepared to wait indefinitely. It had turned down attractive offers for its shareholding, and this block of ABPC shares was costing it about £400 000 a year more to finance than the dividends from the shares themselves: otherwise EMI, as the dominant shareholder, could no doubt have afforded to wait. At the same time, it began to look as though ITA was prepared to take a more reasonable line with EMI, having made its point of principle back in April. But the board of ABPC was less favourably disposed. Sir Joseph Lockwood put his bid proposal to the ABPC board in early December 1968. He received a firm rejection from the ABPC directors, who said they wished to stay independent – there was no rival suitor whom they wanted to encourage.

The timing of EMI's bid was determined by the opportunity to examine the former relationships between Rediffusion and ABPC, and ITA and Thames Television. EMI took the view, which in the event proved justified, that Thames Television going on to an operational basis, plus the fact that since April EMI had sold off its theatrical agency business, would together induce a change of mind by ITA. For the rest, EMI made it clear to ITA that it would give any reasonable assurance of Thames Television's continuing independence, and that it would put on the Thames board only those directors who were not concerned with EMI's leisure business. It added, for good measure, that it was prepared to divest itself of its remaining theatrical agency business. (This last move was intended to answer the criticism that a full merger between EMI and ABPC would give the group control of an artist in all of his activities – as agent, record company, theatre manager, and theatrical or television impresario.)

Bingo Deal

It was soon apparent to EMI that a happily negotiated merger with ABPC was ruled out. The issue, it seems, was precipitated by ABPC's decision to acquire three bingo companies, for the issue of 500000 ordinary shares. Negotiations for this takeover had been under way for some time, and bingo was to prove profitable. But the EMI directors had their reservations about the deal and they did not favour the issue of a block of shares at that stage of the company's development. Therefore, early in December, Sir Joseph Lockwood decided to open what proved to be a sharp two-month takeover fight.

EMI's first offer was probably pitched too low. For the shares which EMI did not own, Sir Joseph Lockwood offered one ordinary share plus 30p loan stock for every ABPC 25p ordinary. The offer was conditional on acceptance from sufficient shareholders to give EMI full voting control of ABPC. EMI also made public that it accepted that ITA would require Thames Television to be run by people of whom it approved; EMI stated that it would be prepared to consider any arrangements which ITA might put forward to this end. Within twenty-four hours, Sir Philip Warter and Mr Clark sent notice of their formal rejection of the EMI offer, and then followed the usual pause while EMI, along with its financial advisers, Lazards, prepared the full details of its bid. This formal offer appeared about a fortnight later, and raised a point of interest which brought some confusion with the City's Takeover Panel.

EMI repeated that it would close its offer when it controlled over 50 per cent of the voting capital of ABPC and it made it clear that it might decide not to extend the offer beyond the date (9 January or later) on which this condition was satisfied. Sir Joseph Lockwood's reasoning was straightforward enough; he saw no reason why he should offer attractive terms to shareholders who held back and simply waited until the issue was clear. The Takeover Panel, at one stage, endorsed Sir Joseph's view, but later backed down when some members argued that Sir Joseph's plan might result in ABPC shareholders being treated in a different manner from others. In the meantime, Sir Philip Warter and Mr Clark were busy talking to their own financial advisers, Robert Fleming, investment bankers, and to Kleinwort Benson, merchant bankers, who had many successful takeover defences to their credit. The ABPC defence appeared over the new year; it was long, comprehensive and, towards an EMI merger, utterly negative. Sir Philip put forward four reasons why he and the board opposed the EMI bid:

(a) EMI was not offering sufficient of its ordinary capital in relation to the two companies' profits;
(b) ABPC shareholders' dividends were reduced under the EMI alternative, compared with the plans being put forward by ABPC;
(c) ABPC had stronger asset backing than EMI;
(d) ABPC had cash resources available for further development which were not reflected in the offer.

These forecasts were accompanied by a detailed analysis of future profits, an explanation that management developments had taken place before the sale of the Warner holdings to EMI, together with an analysis of the £4 million cash holdings which ABPC had available for future planning. ABPC also interjected the earlier point which had arisen over Thames Television, namely that ITA had powers to alter the status of Thames Television if EMI gained control of more than 25 per cent of the Corporation. Sir Philip's statement also underlined how co-operation between the two companies, since EMI had withdrawn its first offer in the spring, had been less than fully harmonious. Sir Philip described, though he did not explain, the five months time lag between ABPC agreeing to take on two EMI directors and the appointment of Mr Read and Mr Delfont. Sir Philip also told shareholders how he had asked Mr Read and Mr Delfont to resign after the EMI offer had appeared, but they had declined to do so.

The first two points in Sir Philip's defence could clearly be countered by EMI through an improvement in the total value of the bid and in the equity content. The merit of Sir Philip's last two points, the size of ABPC assets and the available cash resources, hinged very much on the ABPC management. It was here that the ABPC defence showed its weakest point. The Corporation had not made any great impact in the City as an entertainment business, while its profit and dividend record had hardly put ABPC into the growth category. The principal new move by the ABPC board since the Second World War had been a skilful investment in commercial television, during the early years when substantial profits were still to be made. Other new ventures such as pay-television and bowling had not prospered. The 1968 deal with Technicolor, which brought ABPC a total holding of 30 per cent in the company, represented no more than a reshuffling of assets by the sale to Technicolor of ABPC's former interest in colour processing laboratories. ABPC seemed a first generation company, where the development of new management would be important. As the final shot in its fight for independence, ABPC proposed a free share issue. This, of course, made no alteration to the underlying financial situation, but the amount of new ABPC stock in existence meant that EMI would find it harder, as a matter of tactics, to carry through a successful offer.

Terms Improved

Faced by ABPC's cheerful forecasts of rising profits, EMI substantially improved its offer. It now gave ABPC shareholders an alternative which consisted of, for every ABPC share, either one EMI share plus 60p of loan stock (against 30p previously) or an all equity offer of 1·2 EMI shares for every share in ABPC. This latter alternative was clearly intended to meet Sir Philip Warter's complaint that the equity content of the bid did not match ABPC's relative contribution of profits. EMI repeated that it would declare its offer unconditional, in other words, that its acceptance of holders' shares would be irrevocable, as soon as it had acquired voting control of

ABPC, although the date was necessarily put back another week at this point to 16 January. EMI's improved offer was announced on 7 January, but it brought a chilly reply from ABPC, whose directors promised a further letter, to be posted in six days' time, which would contain reasons for their maintained stand against EMI, including a forecast of still higher profits and dividends.

This letter duly appeared as promised and featured Sir Philip Warter's firm statement that the revised terms from EMI were 'completely unacceptable'. In his earlier circular, Sir Philip had forecast profits of not less than £5 million for the year ending March 1969 and indicated that ABPC would raise dividends from 33·33 per cent to 50 per cent. The Treasury had explicitly excluded companies faced by a takeover situation from the normal 3·5 per cent limit on dividend increases imposed by the incomes policy. In his second circular, Sir Philip set out an even more attractive picture for the period beyond the current year; profits, he said, for the year 1969–70 should be a minimum of £5·6 million and the directors 'would be disappointed' if the actual income was not 'much nearer to' £6 million. The dividend which had just been raised to 50 per cent was projected at 56 per cent and Sir Philip spent some time explaining the group's property activities which 'now justify recognition as an additional section of the group's trading operations'. He looked to extra profits over the next three years of at least £1 million, of which he expected about £200 000 would appear in 1969–70. On top of all this, he expected capital gains from the redevelopment of cinema and other properties.

This represented about as much as the ABPC directors could reasonably forecast, and EMI had to pause to think yet again. For one thing, ABPC was resisting unusually vigorously. In many takeovers, particularly under the new rules, the potential victim is in a position to resist strongly. Second, it was also clear that EMI was being hampered by the exchange of views with ITA.

But ABPC had fired most of its ammunition. It had been helped by a merchant bank particularly successful in defending boards against bids, Kleinwort Benson, but the acceptability of its profit forecasts depended on their credibility, which in turn rested on ABPC's record. EMI had started with 25 per cent of the equity, and it began to buy through the market. This is a perfectly legitimate operation for a bidder, provided he does not pay more than his offer price, though he suffers from the technical drawback that it tends to maintain the stock market price of the 'victim's' shares. During the bid, EMI acquired for cash a total of 8 per cent of ABPC's ordinary shares, giving a 33 per cent head start. ABPC had produced its profit estimates for the coming two years, so EMI countered with estimates for 1968–69 and 1969–70. For the later year, Sir Joseph and his colleagues looked to £16·5 million. These forecasts, backed by EMI's growth record, finally decided the issue.

From then on, the last stages of the battle followed quickly. On 22 January 1969, Lazards and Morgan Grenfell, who were acting on behalf of EMI published the offer. Allowing that ABPC had doubled its share capital, EMI now offered the alternative of one share plus £1·5 loan stock or 1·33 ordinary shares for every ABPC share. Three days later, Sir Philip Warter issued his rejection; Sir Philip's colleagues still thought the EMI bid was 'inadequate' and they stressed that their profit forecast had been prepared on a 'conservative' basis. To support their enthusiasm, the ABPC directors quoted estimates for future profits apart from television: against £2·35 million in 1968, they estimated £3·86 million in 1969 and a range between £4·75 million and £5 million for 1970. Growth, said Sir Philip, was going to come from the logical development of existing activities and exploitation of the group's strong asset position. But for all ABPC's brave words, just five days later, EMI had won.

Stock Market Buying

Acceptances were coming in, and EMI was busy buying in the market. On 28 January, EMI bought no less than 562 000 shares in ABPC through the stock exchange. By the beginning of that week, acceptances had brought EMI to around a 45 per cent holding in ABPC; its aim in buying through the stock market was to move over the crucial 51 per cent level, which would bring control and on which EMI's offer formally depended. On the morning of 29 January, EMI's bankers again bought ABPC shares on a large scale, but in the afternoon their buying halted. The City took this, rightly, as a sign that EMI had won. On 30 January, EMI's bankers announced formal victory; EMI had received acceptances for some 5·1 million shares, equivalent to 17·7 per cent of ABPC's capital. Before the offer, EMI held 8 million shares, equal to a further 24·2 per cent, and during the offer EMI had bought just over 2·75 million units, equal to a further 8·35 per cent. At that point, EMI held 16·6 million units in ABPC, equal to 50·3 per cent of the ordinary capital. Acceptances finally approached 60 per cent. EMI had won and it extended its offer until mid February.

Immediately after EMI's success, talks started about the future of Thames Television, with EMI agreeing to sell a small percentage of ABPC's controlling holding to a group acceptable to ITA. But the final echoes of the battle had still to die away. Sir Philip Warter declined to endorse the EMI bid. Writing to ABPC's shareholders on 3 February, he conceded that some shareholders might now wish to accept the offer and urged them to consult their advisers; but his support was not forthcoming.

Once EMI had gained control of ABPC, major new development plans got under way, whose full scope will emerge over the years ahead. Within two months, EMI disposed of the bingo business and made clear its aim was to concentrate the future development of ABPC on film production and cinemas. Nat Cohen, the producer who had started the *Carry On* comedy series of postwar films, became a director of ABPC, and in May, the appointment of Bryan Forbes, the film director and writer, as head of production for ABPC was announced. Bernard Delfont, installed as ABPC's chief executive, was determined completely to revise ABPC's role in feature films. In June, EMI revealed a plan to develop the 250-strong chain of ABPC theatres.

The success of the bid for ABPC, followed later that year by the acquisition of Associated Fire Alarms and Minerva Fire Defence Systems, led to the idea that EMI had set out on a course of takeovers. In fact, the bids for AFA and Minerva were intended specifically to mobilize, for commercial uses, capabilities which had been developed for military purposes and, even more important, to develop marketing targets for EMI's electronic and industrial operations.

But it was ABPC which transformed EMI. When Sir Joseph addressed shareholders while presenting the 1969 accounts (for the last time as chief executive of EMI), he explained that the enlarged group had been operating at an annual sales level of some £200 million with before tax profits in excess of £19 million. By any standards, EMI had now become a major, international, entertainment organization. Before the acquisition of ABPC, two-thirds of EMI interests were abroad, of which one-third was in the US and one-third elsewhere in the world. The group possessed record companies in some thirty-nine countries, and while overseas entertainment interests were small, the purchase of ABPC was intended to act as a springboard for such development.

In early 1970, this group was managed through a simple and effective board structure. Sir Joseph Lockwood, who retired in November 1969 as chief executive, was chairman. Looking back over the period since May 1954 when he joined EMI, Sir Joseph Lockwood noted that the value of EMI shares had increased 12·4 times, that sales had grown from £32 million to £176 million, and profits from £1·1 million to £17·6 million, and the payroll from 28 300 to 41 900 – by any standards, the transformation of a large industrial company. Of the thirteen members of the parent board four were non-executive, including Lord Shawcross and Sir Ian Jacob, the former head of the BBC; John Read was chief executive heading a team of six executive directors; Bill Stanford was overseas managing director plus four others controlling British electronic and industrial operations, records, and entertainment. There were two overseas directors, the chairman of Capitol and the chairman of EMI's Australian company.

Sir Joseph Retires

Sir Joseph Lockwood had decided to cease being chief executive when he reached sixty-five. He had also taken on the growingly arduous job of chairman of the IRC. John Read, who succeeded him, is fourteen years Lockwood's junior. A wartime naval officer, Read joined Ford in 1946 and moved through finance, marketing, and general management to become sales director. He joined EMI in 1965, and became heir apparent when Sir John Wall moved to the Post Office. Read's principal achievements so far have been to set up a new management structure at EMI and to master-mind the bid for ABPC.

Addressing New York investment analysts early in 1969, when victory in the ABPC battle had become clear, John Read explained EMI's plans. First, through the Grade Organization, he believed that EMI had the skills 'to inject a lot of energy and know-how' into ABPC. 'Basically this has been a stagnant company and I believe that we can inject a lot of new ideas, and supply aggressive management direction which it certainly needs.' Second, ABPC gave EMI a much larger place in the leisure industry with increased strength to deal with artists and the general entertainment world, plus a base for expansion into Europe and Australia. Third, the acquisition of ABPC brought the useful financial advantage of increasing the proportion of profits earned in Britain. This was of considerable potential benefit to EMI, given the difficulties and tax problems often encountered in remitting profits from abroad, notably the developing countries. Chief among these overseas interests remained the 72 per cent holding in Capitol Industries; Capitol's 1968 figures, after an impressive growth record, were clouded because of a once-for-all adjustment to the changeover from mono records. The industry had abandoned mono for stereo records in July 1967. As records in the US are sold on a sale-or-return basis, this led to an avalanche of records being sent back to the manufacturers after the Christmas sales of 1967. Capitol also suffered from the 1969–70 recession.

John Read also explained in New York that EMI looked for increased profitability from its existing interests, without heavy investment, but through 'better management, more vigorous control of our costs, and a progressive operating force'. Acquisitions, particularly on the electronics side, also figure in EMI's planning. In Britain, he explained, there exists a host of small electronics companies, specialists in their particular areas. To stimulate concentration, EMI bought SE Laboratories, and two companies in connectors and marine radar from a group in financial difficulties. EMI also invested in BMF Instruments of Philadelphia to give an outlet for the products of SE Laboratories.

EMI's third objective is to increase its strength worldwide. EMI's great strength lies in its overseas network. EMI's overseas interests are partly concerned with records – though in Australia it holds a large position in the television and radio business, as well as in commercial and military electronics. But in many countries, such as Germany, EMI relies on records and the plan over a few years is to move into the electronics business there. How far can EMI go? Its overwhelming strength is that it is now established in

96

major growth businesses: records, electronics, cinemas, television, tape, and entertainment. One City estimate suggests that this combination could realize an annual growth of some 7 per cent; that would indicate a profit potential of perhaps £28 million.

Probably the greatest interest will centre on how EMI deals with the problems of the film industry in which it now has a major investment through ABPC plus some smaller interests. The background admittedly is not encouraging: nearly 2500 cinemas have closed over the past ten years and four-fifths of cinema audiences have stayed away – often at home to watch television. Film production, too, has started to contract from perhaps seventy to eighty films a year in Britain to barely forty; ABPC led the move away from film production. When this analysis was written in autumn 1970, EMI was not finding the film business easy going, but a final verdict cannot be passed for some time yet.

EMI has established itself, under Lockwood's and Read's guidance, as one of the most successful leisure businesses in the world. The next few years will show whether EMI can succeed in its self-appointed major task of reviving Britain's film industry.

France's Fiercest Bid Battle

Takeover bids hit France with full force at Christmas 1968. Until then, that Anglo-Saxon institution had been comparatively little known; but the bid by Boussois-Souchon-Neuvesel for Saint-Gobain compressed into a few weeks many of the lessons which had been learned in Britain and the US over the previous twenty years. Major takeovers came to France as late as 1964, in the bid handled by Lazards for a US group which tried to gain control of Franco-Wyoming. In November 1966, a struggle took place for the firm Claude Pazet Visseaux, when International Telephone and Telegraph, General Electric of the US and Philips all sought to gain control and each of them put its plans to the Ministry of Finance. The battle ended without a public takeover, when ITT formed an association with Air Liquide, which already held 15 per cent of the share capital. France, during 1962, saw a total of 1320 mergers, rising to 1590 in 1965, and to 1752 in 1967. Among the best known were the links between Renault and Peugeot, the alliance between Fiat and Citroen, and the far reaching steel industry regrouping which involved Wendel-Sidelor and Mosellane de Siderurgerie.

BSN and Saint-Gobain were the largest glass producers in continental Europe. BSN, the smaller, had become the biggest producer of window glass in the world; Pilkingtons of Britain held a 3 per cent stake in the company and one of the Pilkington board sat as a director on BSN. Saint-Gobain, with a turnover four times as large, claimed no less than 22 per cent of all glass sales throughout the free world. Directly or indirectly, Saint-Gobain controlled seventy factories in Europe, the US, and Brazil. Saint-Gobain was also one of the most prestigious of French companies: it had been founded in 1665 by Colbert as part of his plan to make France, under Louis XIV, selfsufficient in key industries. It took its name from a chateau which had been named after an Irish monk. Saint-Gobain earned its place in history by building the mirrors for the famous Hall of Mirrors at the Palace of Versailles. Apart from its dominant position in France (only in window glass did it hold a minority market share), Saint-Gobain was unusual in holding a major place in international markets, including the US, as the table shows:

Saint-Gobain's Market Shares

	Plate glass %	Window glass %	Hollow glass %
France	64	27	35
Germany	90	16	
Italy	50	28	28
Spain	98	56	47
Sweden		51	
US	45	14	

[Source: Hartemann and Ducousset]

BSN was of more recent vintage, having reached its current position as recently as 1966 through the merger of Glaces de Boussois with the Verrerie Souchon-Neuvesel. Long before, and after, that merger, there was extensive co-operation between BSN and Saint-Gobain. In Germany, the two companies had a joint sales organization for exports, and in Spain, a joint company for all business. In France, they had a joint venture split fifty-fifty, for window glass and plate glass for private houses. BSN was also interested in two of Saint-Gobain's most profitable subsidiaries, Fibreglass and Triplex. In France, the two companies had approximately equal shares of the important glass-bottle market: their European sales of flat glass were split approximately 85 to 15 in favour of Saint-Gobain, and the reverse proportions for window glass.

Only six weeks before it launched the bid for Saint-Gobain, BSN took over Tselglas which gave it a key position in window glass in Germany. By that time, BSN commanded about two-thirds of French production of window glass, and one-third of plate glass; it handled about half French production of bottle glass and, thanks to its links with Evian covered nearly one-third of mineral water output. In France, BSN controlled eleven factories, three for float glass and eight for bottle glass. Its turnover was broken down as follows: building 33 per cent, food 35 per cent, table glass 7 per cent, automobile glass 9 per cent, medical 7 per cent, other 9 per cent. Overseas, BSN had built up a major position in Belgium, with an effective monopoly of window glass and about half the market for plate glass. In Germany, BSN held 80 per cent of window-glass production, in Benelux a virtual monopoly of window glass, in Spain about 25 per cent of the window-glass market, and in Brazil about 30 per cent. BSN followed a policy of disposing of interests which it thought would show less than maximum profitability. In this way, it sold off a stake in Sediver to French electrical interests and a holding in Sovirel to Corning Glass of the US.

Boussois, which had been set up in 1908, specialized in window glass. In the 'fifties, Boussois extended its interests in Belgium and in 1961 took over the Belgium firm Mecaniver, which in turn brought control of a number of international businesses. The following year, Boussois acquired the float-glass licence from Pilkington for the Common Market. Souchon-Neuvesel had specialized in hollow glass, a sector characterized by the existence of a large number of small companies. In postwar years, Souchon-Neuvesel set about taking over many of these with names like Fleury, Verrerie de Folembray, and many others. Yet by the late 'sixties, the two companies, BSN and Saint-Gobain, presented a contrasting picture to the outside world. Over the previous decade, the profits of Saint-Gobain had risen modestly from F3·98 to F5·81 per share; at the same time, the profits of BSN had nearly trebled, from F9·02 to F25·22. Shareholders of Saint-Gobain had undergone an even more depressing experience. During the same period, the value of their holdings had dropped from F178 to F147; by contrast, the value of BSN shares had trebled from F326 to F975.

Contrast in Chairmen

The contrast between the two companies was epitomized by the two chairmen. As head of Saint-Gobain was Count Arnaud de Vogüé, a member of one of the aristocratic families which had run Saint-Gobain throughout its entire history. At the head of BSN was an entirely different figure, Antoine Riboud, often taken in France as the prototype of the successful Anglo-Saxon manager. Riboud, born in 1918 in Lyons, was the son of a banker. His family had a substantial interest in the firm of Souchon-Neuvesel, which it had helped to found. Riboud joined the firm and quickly showed that he was different from the traditional members of the conservative glass families of Lyons, bringing aggression and zest to an otherwise peaceful business. In 1956, he became President and Director-General of Souchon-Neuvesel, and one of the key figures in the French glass industry; ten years later, he became chief executive of BSN.

Count Arnaud de Vogüé presented a great contrast. De Vogüé was born, in 1904, of one of the most aristocratic families in France. His grandfather had been chief executive of Saint-Gobain and the Marquis Melchior de Vogüé had been one of the expounders of Russian literature in France and had joined the Académie Française. From the Sorbonne, de Vogüé joined the Société Indochinoise de Plantation de Héveas. After a distinguished war record, he succeeded the Baron Hely D'Oissel at Saint-Gobain in 1952. By contrast with Riboud, de Vogüé aimed for diversification. His aim was not to reduce the role of glass in Saint-Gobain's affairs, but to give it an important, but secondary, place. Two of de Vogüé's moves showed the way his mind was working: an early deal with Shell-Berre and, in 1962, the formation, with Pechiney, the large non-ferrous metal group, of a jointly owned company.

Saint-Gobain was in the unusual position of having its capital of 11·5 million shares spread among a large number of shareholders. These 200 000

100

shareholders, coupled with the company's apparent financial vulnerability, were to plunge Saint-Gobain into France's most sensational takeover.

The origins of the battle went back to 1965 when Paul Lepercq, head of Saint–Gobain's important US business, put to Arnaud de Vogüé the proposition that Saint-Gobain should take over BSN as part of a general restructuring of the European glass industry. At the same time, Lepercq suggested that Antoine Riboud should take over as director general of Saint-Gobain from de Vogüé who was due to retire in four years. Arnaud de Vogüé turned down Lepercq's suggestion to make Riboud chief executive: he took the view that this appointment would provoke opposition among other directors and senior executives.

But Saint-Gobain was about to run into management problems. Ray Grandgeorge was soon to retire as chief executive. De Vogüé named d'Argenlieu, an insider from Saint-Gobain, as chief executive in succession to Grandgeorge; but even before the latter retired, d'Argenlieu fell seriously ill. The problem of succession now became acute; a number of senior French civil servants were suggested, and Valery Giscard d'Estaing, the distinguished former Finance Minister, was even named as a possible candidate. It was only in 1967 that de Vogüé found the man, Edmond Pirlot, who possessed the qualities which seemed to him essential, an engineering and administrative background coupled with acceptable standing.

These problems, which were naturally no secret in the higher reaches of French banking and industry, helped to direct attention to Saint-Gobain. One group which took more than a passing interest was Lazard Frères, the French opposite number of the powerful Wall Street and City of London banking houses. As far back as 1962, it had pondered a takeover of Saint-Gobain possibly in alliance with a US glass group, but this idea was dropped. In 1966, it took up the idea again, this time more seriously. Lazard suggested a merger to Riboud, who had just put together BSN by merging Souchon-Neuvesel with Boussois.

Change of View

Riboud declined as he thought the deal was too big and, at that point, a takeover of Saint-Gobain did not fit in with his own plans. There was a further attempt the following year to arrange a meeting between de Vogüé and Riboud to encourage BSN to take an interest in a possible takeover, but once more Riboud declined. But over the next twelve months, Riboud changed his mind. The reasons for this are not entirely clear. Perhaps Riboud came to see the appeal of the Lazard plan; perhaps the integration of BSN succeeded faster than he had hoped; perhaps he was influenced by the attack on the French glass market which was being launched by Glaverbel of Belgium in which BSN held a large but not controlling interest. Riboud hit on the plan of countering Glaverbel's competition by a merger with Saint-Gobain. This idea appealed to him so much that in May 1968 he went to see the Prime Minister, Georges Pompidou, in order to discuss an overall restructuring of the French glass industry. Riboud's timing was unfortunate; the May riots pushed other questions into the background and led to Pompidou's own departure from the government. Riboud's plan thus lost any hope of official backing at that time, but Lazard itself, and especially one of its partners, Pierre David-Weill, still pursued the merger scheme.

Pierre David-Weill was the grandson of Alexandre Weill one of the founders of Lazard who was himself a cousin of the Alexandre Lazard who settled in New Orleans in the 1840s. Between the two world wars, Alexandre's son, David Weill, took charge of French Lazard and arranged, among many other deals, the Michelin family's takeover of Citroen. It was David Weill's son, Pierre David-Weill, and grandson, Michel, now a director of BSN, who played the key roles in the BSN takeover.

Once he had accepted the Lazard plan, Riboud proposed a full merger of BSN and Saint-Gobain to de Vogüé, but the latter declined. Instead, de Vogüé offered BSN a participation in Saint-Gobain's plate-glass operation in Germany. This represented a considerable concession by de Vogüé, but Riboud now believed that a full merger was imperative. He expounded his views at a dinner with de Vogüé in September 1968, and pointed to the far reaching changes now affecting the industry, such as Vittel, the large French mineral water group, switching from glass to plastic bottles. Once again, de Vogüé took a cool view of Riboud's merger plans. Riboud made one last effort at a dinner on 4 October between himself and Edmond Pirlot, now designated to take over as chief executive at Saint-Gobain. De Vogüé held strong views on monopoly: 'Monopoly makes the ideal prey for nationalization, and puts an end to the dynamism which is produced by competition.' But Pirlot, unlike de Vogüé, accepted the logic behind Riboud's plan for a complete merger. He asked, however, for two to three years' grace to enable him to take stock at Saint-Gobain. For Riboud, such a delay was out of the question. When the dinner broke up just after midnight, it was clear that Saint-Gobain would not agree to a full scale merger at that time with BSN. That dinner represented a turning-point for Riboud. He could use BSN's cash resources either for development, or to attempt a takeover of Saint-Gobain, which was bound to be resisted. Many of his friends and advisers pressed him to go ahead with a bid. One of these was Jerome Seydoux, son of a former diplomat, whose mother was a Schlumberger, and who represented the powerful merchant bank, Neuflize Schlumberger Mallet. Paul Lepercq also supported the idea, as did the principal executives of BSN.

On 20 October, Riboud lunched with Pierre and Michel David-Weill and Jean Guyot, a Lazard director, at the bank. He told them that he would be interested in considering a plan for a complete merger between BSN and Saint-Gobain. From that point onwards, the planning at Lazard was in the

102

hands of three men: David-Weill, Seydoux, and Guyot. The Lazard team, having investigated a large number of possibilities, finally settled on a convertible offer by BSN. A share exchange would have been simpler, but there were legal problems. BSN and Lazard finally agreed on an offer of F230 of BSN convertible stock for each Saint-Gobain share, compared with the then market price of around F140; the convertible was to carry a 4·5 per cent interest rate. Riboud did not envisage a bid for the entire capital of Saint-Gobain. With hindsight, this would have been a riskier, though possibly more appealing, plan. Riboud simply wanted to acquire a substantial shareholding which would ensure effective control, but would not endanger the position of BSN itself.

Lazard's plan rested essentially on the belief that some 30 per cent of the equity in Saint-Gobain could be attracted in a bid. To start with, perhaps 5 per cent of the Saint-Gobain equity was already held by friends of Riboud. The obvious threat to the BSN-Lazard plan was a counter-attack by massive buying of Saint-Gobain shares through the Bourse; that would require, it was estimated, between £60 million and £70 million, a figure which was ironically to prove almost exactly right. Lazard and BSN decided that no one with this sort of money was likely to intervene: the big US glass companies, for example, were reckoned to be non-starters on political grounds. This was a reasonable but, in the event, crucially mistaken forecast.

Final Meeting

The last meeting, for a long time to come, between Riboud and de Vogüé took place on 8 November. Riboud stressed again the case for a merger and emphasized that BSN could not be expected to stand by while Saint-Gobain developed its float-glass plans. De Vogüé simply repeated his former offer of a 15 per cent share stake in Saint-Gobain's German factory. Lazard had, by this time, produced a detailed analysis of the shareholdings in Saint-Gobain. They divided holders of the 11·5 million shares into three groups:

(a) Financial institutions;

(b) A large number of small holders aged fifty or more (often former employees of the company);

(c) Younger shareholders under forty-five.

They found that no less than 30000 shareholders in Saint-Gobain held fewer than 9 shares each, another 30000 between 10 and 19 shares, while 40000 held between 20 and 50 shares. Only 587 individuals held 500 shares or more each in Saint-Gobain, and about one-third of all shareholders lived in the Paris area. A large number of these holdings were in the names of leading deposit banks who were often responsible for their management. Thus the Credit Lyonnais, the leading French bank, represented 14 per cent of Saint-Gobain's shares, the Banque Nationale de Paris another 15 per cent, and the Société Générale another 8 per cent. Another 15 per cent of the shares

103

was held in stockbrokers' names. In all, no less than 52 per cent of Saint-Gobain's share capital was owned or managed by financially sophisticated institutions, to whom Lazard thought an attractive offer would appeal.

On 31 October, the battle came a stage nearer when Paul Lepercq, president of Saint-Gobain's US interests, handed in his resignation. Many of his colleagues at Saint-Gobain took the view that this reflected disappointment at the appointment of Edmond Pirlot as chief executive – Pirlot had at one time served on Lepercq's staff in the US. But the reason for Lepercq's resignation was more fundamental, and rested on his view that Riboud was right, in that a merger between BSN and Saint-Gobain was vital for the future of the French glass industry. By 6 December, Riboud and Lazard were ready to launch their takeover. As a first step, they decided to build up their holding in Saint-Gobain to between 10 and 15 per cent by buying in the stock market. This was bound to alert the Saint-Gobain board, but they considered the risk was inevitable. Before that, Riboud and Lazard thought it essential to sound out the government. On 10 December, Riboud himself visited the Ministry of Finance. Officials did not show any great enthusiasm for the idea of a contested takeover, perhaps this smacked too much of Anglo-Saxon behaviour, but Riboud was assured that the Ministry would remain neutral. Two days later, on the afternoon of 12 December, David-Weill was due to meet de Vogüé in New York. Rumours had by now begun about a possible bid for Saint-Gobain. On 18 December, the operations got under way; Riboud, along with David-Weill, Guyot, and Seydoux, called upon Jean Reyre of the Banque de Paris et des Pays Bas. They asked Reyre whether he would join forces with them in making a public bid for 3·36 million shares in Saint-Gobain. De Vogüé was a director of Paribas, but Reyre decided to place all the resources of his powerful financial institution behind BSN and Lazard. On 20 December, the board of BSN gave formal approval to Riboud's plan by endorsing the creation of the BSN convertible stock which could be used to buy shares in Saint-Gobain. The BSN-Lazard plan was now moving ahead, but just before it became public the attackers hit their first snag.

The BSN scheme had to be ratified by the French stock exchange, but Pierre Chatenet, president of the operations commission of the stock exchange, had some reservations. As a result, Lazard and BSN did not receive formal approval from the stock exchange until 3 January, by which time the bid had long been a public issue.

On 21 December, the takeover plan finally became public. An official statement from Riboud announced that BSN was seeking a holding of 28·5 per cent in Saint-Gobain by offering F230 of convertible stock for each share in Saint-Gobain; the statement confirmed that this convertible would pay interest at 4·5 per cent, and at the end of three years it could be turned into BSN shares in the ratio of two for nine. This assumed a minimum market value of F108 for BSN shares. To the extent that the stock was not converted, it would be redeemed over twelve years by drawings on a random basis at a price of F242, compared with F230 nominal value. The initial BSN announcement carried no details about its existing shareholdings in Saint-Gobain. Looking back, it is possible that BSN and Lazard committed a tactical error, for the revelation of a large shareholding in Saint-Gobain at this stage might have convinced many small shareholders. Riboud was also concerned about publicity; he needed to get his views across to a large number of Saint-Gobain shareholders and to the French public in general. BSN itself was not that widely known, and Riboud rightly feared that a full scale takeover battle might prove hard for the French public to appreciate. He talked to Havas, the public relations agency. One of his main advisers was Jean-Jacques Servan-Schreiber, owner and editor of *L'Express* and well known in France and abroad as the author of *The American Challenge*, an analysis of US companies' penetration into Europe.

Public Image

Publicity began to play an important part in the takeover. On 31 December, Saint-Gobain with its advisers, Publicis, helped by the newspaper *France Soir*, organized an opinion poll. This showed 43·6 per cent thought Saint-Gobain had a non-dynamic image, though 40 per cent took exactly the opposite view. Asked about the takeover offer which had been announced ten days before, 38 per cent thought that the shareholders would accept, but 62 per cent thought they would decline. A little later, Havas, acting for BSN, organized a survey which covered January 7, 8, and 9. This suggested that no less than 75 per cent of Saint-Gobain shareholders would say no to BSN, that 17 per cent would accept, while the remaining 8 per cent were undecided.

These surveys also pointed to the factors working against BSN, such as the method of payment in convertible stock which seemed satisfactory only to 15 per cent of shareholders in Saint-Gobain. BSN itself emerged as little known, and there was a sentimental attachment to Saint-Gobain which is neatly summed up by one old lady's now famous remark, made during a visit to one of Saint-Gobain's factories: 'One inherits Saint-Gobain shares, one doesn't sell them.'

Riboud decided not to make any further public statement until the second week of January. He and his advisers agreed to keep publicity to the minimum until then. Lazard had been greatly impressed by a study carried out by J. Walter Thompson in London of the takeover by GEC of AEI, a major contested battle in which the bidder won. This suggested that it was letters to shareholders which carried most weight. That argument almost certainly represented less than the full truth about the GEC-AEI battle, and it was to prove wide of the mark in the Saint-Gobain affair. As the aggressor, Riboud's main hope of success lay in combating a large, prestigious, though not over-successful, French industrial concern through keeping up a barrage of propaganda. Yet Riboud's only public move was to meet the trade unions on 23 December to assure them that the merger, if it succeeded, would not cause any redundancies.

In the event, Riboud delayed his speech until 13 January. It was a most carefully prepared statement on which he spent most of the previous week. So elaborate were the preparations that on Saturday, 11 January, all Riboud's close friends met him at Versailles to go over the speech and polish it to the last detail. By then, unfortunately, Riboud was well on the way to defeat. But the press conference, attended by between 300 and 400 journalists, bankers, and businessmen, proved a considerable success. That afternoon, Riboud also spoke to a meeting of stockbrokers and financial analysts which again proved a success. Riboud's press conference concentrated on the need for competition, and for enlarging France's glass industry in order to stand against European and US rivals.

De Vogüé, with a nice sense of timing, launched a counter-attack on that same day and announced that Saint-Gobain's 1968 profits had risen by 35 per cent over those for 1967 to reach F130 million. The Saint-Gobain directors also forecast that profits should double from then until 1971, and they announced a one for four scrip issue. It was becoming clear that de Vogüé had found sufficient funds to mount a counter-attack. Jean Reyre of the Banque de Paris put the view to Riboud that the offer should be either increased or abandoned.

The Riboud press conference had boosted the chances of BSN, but the effect was rather less than the BSN camp might have hoped. Of those polled by Publicis, 45 per cent thought that Saint-Gobain shareholders would accept the BSN offer. But a Havas survey showed that 47 per cent thought the one for four scrip issue was of benefit to shareholders, against 23 per cent who thought it was simply a tactical move in the takeover battle.

De Vogüé Counter-Attack

De Vogüé opened his own counter-attack to Riboud on 16 January. In searching through Riboud's speech for a weak point, he pounced on the comment: 'I am devoted to glass.' De Vogüé aimed to show how he, and Saint-Gobain, had wider vistas. At his press conference, de Vogüé arranged for plastic bottles to be brought in and distributed round the room. De Vogüé himself, at the height of the conference, waved a bottle made of plastic for the Vittel mineral water group. (No one mentioned that the plastic had been produced by Solvay of Belgium.) De Vogüé saw, as an integral part of his propaganda, that diversification as opposed to integration was the way that the company should develop.

On 23 January, Lazard tried a final tactical fling by selling Saint-Gobain shares which temporarily pushed the market price down. But this was a last ditch defence. On the following day, a conference was called at Riboud's house, including himself, Jean Reyre, and André Mayer, the prestigious head of Lazard in New York, and one of the most powerful of international bankers. (One bizarre aspect of the whole affair took place on the night of 16–17 January when the BSN office was damaged by a bomb, while on the Boulevard St Germain, Riboud's town flat was also damaged. While the incidents did some damage to BSN and Riboud, they reinforced a typical view that a takeover battle is a rather vulgar affair, and not the way for major companies to proceed.)

Reyre was now for giving up. Mayer also believed that the BSN bid could not succeed but he wanted to try for a compromise. He suggested an agreement to be blessed by either the Prime Minister or the Minister of Finance. Mayer had played a major role in the Citroen-Fiat affair, where Fiat had agreed to modify its original plan to buy control of Citroen for, temporarily at least, a minority participation. Mayer had dealt direct with Couve de Murville during these negotiations and thought that he might induce the Minister to intervene again. On the Saturday, Mayer called on François Xavier Ortoli, the French Finance Minister. Ortoli agreed that a compromise would be desirable and asked Ennemond Bizot, the President of the Banque Nationale de Paris and a personal friend of de Vogüé, to act as arbitrator. Bizot telephoned de Vogüé but received a chilly reply; de Vogüé said that the time for reconciliation was now past. On Sunday, 26 January, a harassed and tired Riboud appeared on French television. He was asked the origin of the F8 million which had allegedly been thrown on the stock market to buy Saint-Gobain shares. At this point, Riboud knew as little as his interrogator. The following day, Riboud and his bankers conceded defeat.

Back on 20 December, the Saint-Gobain directors had believed that a bid was in the offing and had begun making plans accordingly. But no hint of their elaborate work had become apparent until Friday, 27 December. On that day, Jean Yves Alquier, director of public relations at Saint-Gobain, sent out the first letter to shareholders. These letters did not reach many shareholders till the following Monday, but Alquier made sure that the Saint-Gobain reply was known to the French press: *Paris Presse* headlined the Saint-Gobain counter-attack in its issue of Saturday. The tone of the Saint-Gobain counter-attack was so sharp that David-Weill thought it was legally damaging to Lazard. That weekend, Alquier passed on Lazard's feelings both to de Vogüé and Pirlot who were away from Paris; neither of them seemed particularly disturbed. The letter which reached Saint-Gobain shareholders that Monday was sharp enough:

You have learned through the press that BSN has asked you to sell it your shares . . . it is clear that the world-wide reputed technology

107

of Saint-Gobain, the efficiency of its research, the geographical spread and the capacity of its European industrial installations . . . are extremely tempting for a company like BSN which has made less progress in this area.

The letter suggested that Saint-Gobain shareholders were being asked to sell their assets for too small a sum and it also asked what would be the likely value of BSN shares if the deal went through. Saint-Gobain had yet another powerful card to play. On 7 January, Saint-Gobain announced through the press and radio that it was considering legal action against the offer: 'The Company has decided to appeal to the Tribunal of Commerce in Paris to set aside the takeover bid as a violation of French law.' At precisely five minutes to four that same day, just before the close of business, writ servers appeared at Lazard, at the Banque de Paris, and at Neuflize Schlumberger, and handed over a writ from Saint-Gobain; a fourth appeared at BSN's office in the Boulevard Malesherbes. The BSN camp was somewhat concerned about the legal aspects of the takeover; a number of fundamental questions were unresolved, and it was known that Saint-Gobain's advisers included Professor Goldman of Paris, one of the leading specialists in European law. Saint-Gobain's move proved effective, for it induced the BSN bankers and lawyers to pay close attention to each aspect of the bid and it specifically inhibited them from attacking Saint-Gobain.

Propaganda Effort

Saint-Gobain also embarked on what was to prove one of the key planks in its defence, a massive and skilled propaganda effort. No less than 133 000 letters were sent to shareholders, another 36 000 to customers and suppliers, and a further 5000 were sent to lawyers in France. A copy of the newspaper *France Soir*, which contained a discussion (the report of a kind of brains trust, a feature popular in the French press), favourable to Saint-Gobain, was reprinted and 200 000 copies were sent out by the company. One of the most striking features of the takeover counter-attack was the behaviour of de Vogüé himself. Apart from master-minding the financial operations, de Vogüé projected himself into the public eye as a leader of a revitalized Saint-Gobain. De Vogüé appeared in public, while Pirlot organized the internal defences. Pirlot and Alquier (whose department had previously consisted of himself and a secretary) organized groups in the information division to deal with each important sector: shareholders, stock exchange, customers, chambers of commerce, and so on. On 30 December, Saint-Gobain joined with Publicis, who assigned one of its top executives, Gerard Pedraglio, to work full time on Saint-Gobain. One of Publicis' first ideas, put forward by the director general, Claude Marcos, was to invite shareholders to telephone their support to the company. A good deal of press publicity went into this plan and at 8 a.m. on the Thursday after New

Year, Saint-Gobain stood ready to receive telephone calls. By 10 a.m. the Saint-Gobain switchboard was completely jammed; new equipment was brought in and by noon the switchboard was open again. The Publicis men set up a microphone system through which shareholders' questions could be passed on to the appropriate experts involved. The Saint-Gobain specialists (financial, industrial, legal, and so on) worked two to three hour shifts during which they answered a barrage of queries. On the first day, no less than 1800 shareholders telephoned. In all, some 9000 shareholders telephoned Saint-Gobain, most of them to express support for de Vogüé and his board.

On top of all this, another 4000 shareholders wrote to Saint-Gobain's headquarters at Neuilly outside Paris, and de Vogüé arranged that each of them should receive an immediate reply. On Saturday, 18 January, Saint-Gobain held an open day for shareholders at its Neuilly headquarters. This again was a skilful and highly successful operation. Each shareholder was given a large card bearing his name and the title 'Shareholder in Saint-Gobain'. Each Saint-Gobain employee carried a label giving his name and his job; every office on the ground floor at Neuilly was staffed by Saint-Gobain executives ready to answer shareholders' questions.

The shareholders poured in. The highlight of the day came when de Vogüé himself appeared, mixed with the shareholders, and answered questions. As Michel Gabrysiak wrote later, this was the first time that a French industrialist had been treated like a politician or a pop star; and it worked. The most frequent question put to de Vogüé and his staff, was who was buying Saint-Gobain shares in the Bourse? De Vogüé assured shareholders that neither the company nor its subsidiaries had bought any shares.

In all, about 7000 shareholders visited Neuilly. Saint-Gobain also mounted an anti-BSN campaign by mobilizing its own staff. Henry Vivier, one of the senior production executives in the company, impressed on all workers the need to make clear to their friends and relations the prospects of the company and why it was important not to accept the offer from BSN. In this way, another network of supporters was organized throughout France.

The results of this operation showed up in polls of institutions which held Saint-Gobain shares and where BSN had hoped that its sophisticated scheme would meet with considerable support. At the Bank of France in Neuilly, no one, it seemed, would accept the bid. At the Banque Nationale de Paris in the Champs Elysees, the BSN offer again found no takers. In the Credit Lyonnais offices, few said they would accept the takeover; in most offices of the Societe Générale, support was for Saint-Gobain and not for BSN.

After the success of the 'open factory' day at Neuilly, Saint-Gobain organized visits to its factories up and down the country. It set aside Sunday, 12 January; this proved another outstanding success. On that day, it was estimated that no less than 120000 people visited Saint-Gobain factories.

The visitors included a group of schoolboys who had been asked to write an essay on the takeover; a large number of employees' families, who wanted to see where the head of the family worked; and not a few people interested in carrying away a memento of their visit. But overall, Saint-Gobain was able to establish national pride in one of France's largest and most old established industrial groups. Saint-Gobain executives also hinted at the possibility of redundancies if Riboud acquired a large holding in the group. A series of factory-floor resolutions to support Saint-Gobain were introduced along with the following statement:

> To the directors: We transmit to you a motion adopted by the great majority of the personnel and the employees of the factory. We the workers give you our support to safeguard the interests of the employees.

Admittedly, the Chemical Workers' Union made the point that it had taken the threat of a takeover to induce a more co-operative attitude on the part of the Saint-Gobain management (a point also taken by some shareholders), but the overall benefit to the company was considerable.

At the start of the battle, Claude Marcos of Publicis gave his opinion of the odds as six to four in favour of BSN. Skilful newspaper advertising went a long way to redressing this balance. During a seasonally quiet time of year, when large advertising spaces could be obtained at short notice, Saint-Gobain spent some £20000 on advertising in the Paris press and more than £39000 in the provincial press, plus another £30000 on radio advertising.

Legal Difficulties

From the BSN side, neither Riboud nor his advisers seems to have appreciated the strength of Saint-Gobain's public relations counter-attack. They were hampered by legal difficulties, and by some mistaken ideas about the GEC-AEI battle in Britain. They thought BSN could build on the standing of Riboud himself as a modern, efficient figure, though the company itself was little known. Havas sent out letters giving the scope and aims of BSN to 165000 shareholders in Saint-Gobain and a similar number of leading individuals in Paris and the provinces. Advertisements appeared in *Figaro*, the authoritative French daily paper, and *Expansion*, the newly founded business magazine. The crucial decision by Riboud, after the meeting with Havas on 26 December, was to postpone publicity until the middle of January. Of vital interest here were the doubts expressed by BSN's legal advisers.

They argued that BSN had no sure standing by which to appeal to shareholders in Saint-Gobain, and they even hinted that a press conference could raise problems. BSN's bankers were concerned partly at the legal difficulties, and partly at what they considered the rather brash publicity techniques being suggested. The latter view, at least, seems to have been a misjudgement: the BSN camp did not fully realize the scale or likely impact of

Saint-Gobain's efforts. (There is a curious parallel to the ICI-Courtaulds battle, but with the roles of defender and aggressor reversed.) Later, as doubts grew in the BSN camp, Riboud called in the French offshoot of Young and Rubicam, the big US advertising and public relations agency, to join Havas. Functions were split on the basis that Young and Rubicam would produce publicity statements for BSN and Riboud, while Havas would take over all other responsibilities. But Riboud was too late; he was losing the propaganda war and, even more important, he had already lost the war that was being fought through the stock exchange.

While Riboud was realizing his plans for an attack on Saint-Gobain, de Vogüé and his allies were planning a massive, secret counter-offensive whose full details have never been made fully clear. De Vogüé talked to Georges-Picot, head of the Suez Finance Group which had risen from the ashes of the old Suez Canal Company seized by Nasser in 1956. Picot had rebuilt Suez, which had started with assets of a mere £27 million into a major financial complex, rivalling the Banque de Paris et des Pays-Bas – and Picot had carried along Her Majesty's Government as a 20·5 per cent shareholder. For Picot, the success of the BSN bid would have meant victory for one of his major rivals; on the positive side, he believed that Saint-Gobain could be turned into a more successful business through a merger with Suez's own major associate, Pont-à-Mousson. But the only way to defeat Riboud was to buy Saint-Gobain shares through the Paris Bourse. That would represent a deal costing between £60 million and £70 million. It would be easily the biggest stock exchange deal in French history. But that is just what Picot arranged.

Saint-Gobain shares had not proved much comfort to their holders in recent years. Their postwar peak of F450 was reached in 1961; six years later, after an uninspiring profit record, they had sunk to an all time low of F109. The following year, 1968, was happier for Saint-Gobain holders, the shares moved from F145 at the beginning of the year to F165 just before the May riots. Like all leading French shares, Saint-Gobain dropped steeply after the riots to F130. They recovered slowly to F135 to 140 on premature rumours of French devaluation in November (when Monsieur Ortoli became one of the few finance ministers not to carry out a devaluation which had been agreed – the reverse is more usual) and to F145 in the first few days of December 1968.

The share price began to rise as early as 6 December, more than two weeks before Riboud made his bid public. On that day, 28 000 shares changed hands, compared with a normal daily turnover of around 5000. From then on, turnover grew, the price rose, and the rumours multiplied. With hindsight, it looks as though three separate groups were in the market: Riboud and his allies, Picot and his allies, and the speculators. The speculators came out in force, and by helping to push up the Saint-Gobain price, they proved of great help to Picot and de Vogue: the BSN offer, of F230 a share, looked steadily less attractive as the market price rose.

Bourse Frenzy

On 12 December, turnover reached 40000 shares and the price touched F164. A week later, turnover moved up to 115000 shares and the price rose to F185. The following day, 20 December, saw near frenzy on the Bourse. Rumours flooded round the stock exchange that Corning Glass of the US was to bid for Saint-Gobain at F230 a share; within twenty-four hours the rumour was to prove right on price, but wrong on the bidder. That day, no less than 410000 shares were traded, equivalent to 3·5 per cent of Saint-Gobain's entire share capital. The price rose to F204 at one time, then fell back to F190.

Next day, Riboud announced his bid; but from 1 January 1968 until the BSN bid became public, no less than 22 per cent of Saint-Gobain's shares had been sold and bought on the Bourse; about 8 per cent of the shares had changed hands in December alone. Of this 22 per cent, some had been bought by BSN and its allies; a substantial total had been acquired by the Picot group; and a number by speculators.

By the time he launched his bid, therefore, Riboud faced a situation where the ownership of Saint-Gobain had undergone a major change. Over the following weeks, the highly effective propaganda pouring from Saint-Gobain was both undermining Riboud's case and buoying up speculators' hopes. After the Christmas holiday, turnover stayed high and Saint-Gobain shares touched the bid level of F230. During the first week of January, turnover averaged between 50000 and 100000 shares a day and the price fluctuated between F210 and F225. At these prices, as Reyre argued, a bid of F230 was hardly a great attraction. But in the last ten days of January, when it was clear that Riboud had failed to win over Saint-Gobain shareholders, the Suez group moved in on a massive scale. Its tactics made sense: to have launched large scale buying earlier, in the face of possibly substantial support for Riboud, could have left it locked in as a minority with Riboud in effective control. On Friday, 17 January, more than 400000 shares were traded and the Saint-Gobain price crossed the crucial line of F230. The following Tuesday a new record volume of 455000 shares was realized and the price reached F238. Next day, the price declined to F234, but a new peak turnover was established of more than 500000 shares or some F120 million cash.

The man who had handled all this massive buying with skill and discretion was Jacques Simon. In his forties, Simon had become a stockbroker after starting as a junior bank employee. He joined the broking firm of Reimpre and in 1950 became a partner. He took part in some of the best known deals on the Paris stock exchange – in Young bonds and the Parentis boom in Esso in 1954. More significantly, he had acted for the Suez Finance group in its fight against Paribas for control of Credit Industriel et Commerciel. He was also associated with the introduction on the Paris stock exchange of the L'Oreal perfume company and of Moet and Chandon, the champagne producer – a company, incidentally, which was headed by Arnaud de Vogüé's cousin and brother-in-law.

On 24 January, Simon helped to break all stock exchange records. At the opening, Saint-Gobain shares declined to F202, but soon recovered to F217. Simon then announced that he would take all shares that were on offer. He was still being flooded with orders when the Bourse closed at 2.30, and the authorities had to extend trading for another twenty-five minutes in order to accommodate Simon and the Saint-Gobain business. By the end of the day, no less than 859 000 shares had been traded for a total cash consideration of F185 million. This was easily a new record for business in the history of the Paris stock exchange. Since 1 December 1968, therefore, 48 per cent of Saint-Gobain's ordinary capital had changed hands, or roughly 5·5 million shares. Of these, some 4 million had been bought by Simon for his unknown backers. The rest seemed to have been acquired by speculators or by in-investment institutions. Riboud and his allies had by then sold virtually all their holdings, in an unsuccessful attempt to curb the rise in Saint-Gobain's share price. They acknowledged defeat; the formal result of BSN's bid was that a mere 843 000 shares or 8 per cent of Saint-Gobain's share capital were tendered for Riboud's takeover offer.

Third Force

But who was this Third Force, as it had become known on the Bourse? De Vogue stated that it was up to the buyers to tell Saint-Gobain shareholders who they were – a far cry from British and US takeover practice. The Paris Bourse, which had been given the full details, simply stated that no foreign interests were involved. The *Financial Times* named, among others, Shell, the Deutsche Bank, and Moet et Chandon, all of whom denied taking part. Georges-Picot, of Suez Finance, was widely named as the architect of the Bourse operation, though his methods were not wholly clear.

One widely accepted view was that Saint-Gobain itself, helped by Suez Finance, had raised the money in a way which did not run counter to the rules of the French stock exchange and which conformed with the strict letter of the law and with de Vogüé's own denials of the company's own buying. According to some French banking sources, what happened was that Saint-Gobain arranged a facility for some £25 million through a number of European banks. As collateral, Saint-Gobain pledged shares in Saint-Gobain International, the holding company based in Fribourg which controlled its offshoots in Spain, Germany, Belgium, Italy, and other European countries.

It would be satisfying perhaps to record that Saint-Gobain prospered after beating off Riboud and after coming closer to Suez. But life did not go smoothly. Within weeks of winning the right to stay independent, de Vogüé had to face an entirely new sort of industrial problem – an international strike.

Saint-Gobain owned plants in twelve countries, most of them under the control of Saint-Gobain International. The strike action started with a breakdown in wage negotiations in the US subsidiary, while wage negotiations in France and Italy were still proceeding. The International Federation of Chemical and General Workers, based in Geneva and headed by an active secretary-general, Charles Levinson, accused Saint-Gobain of being: 'One of the most secretive and backward companies in the world when it comes to publishing information' and added that it could not 'play groups of workers in one country off against groups in another'. In March 1969, a meeting in Switzerland of union representatives from Saint-Gobain subsidiaries demanded that concessions made to workers in France (following the May riots of 1968) be extended to all the company's factories world wide. The operation proved a striking success for Levinson and the International Federation. A bitter three-week strike in the US was supported in both Germany and Italy. Saint-Gobain made important concessions: in the US, the settlement granted a 30 per cent wage increase over the next three years plus guarantees against technological unemployment; in Germany, two months of negotiations resulted in a 7·5 per cent wage increase, again with protection against unemployment; in Italy, a strike was called but the company conceded union demands four days before the walkout. Rumours also persisted that Saint-Gobain had still to pay off large sums which it had raised to fight off BSN and Riboud. De Vogüé's first move, of which rumours leaked in the spring, and which was completed in July, was to dispose of part of Saint-Gobain's interest in the large joint company which it had developed with Pechiney, in which the two held a fifty-fifty interest. This company, which had become the second largest chemical complex in France, was sold to Rhone Poulenc. Saint-Gobain and Pechiney retained 10 per cent and 39 per cent respectively of their subsidiary, with Rhone Poulenc taking 51 per cent. In July, again, Saint-Gobain confirmed that it was negotiating to sell part of its shares in Sovirel to Corning Glass Works of the US. Corning already owned 49 per cent of Sovirel, and this deal would have generated useful funds for Saint-Gobain. But the French Government intervened; the sale of Sovirel shares to Corning would have given the US company control of the French concern which played a key role in the development of France's Secam colour television system; Sovirel made the highly specialized glass for the tube.

Pont-à-Mousson Merger

In late July, Saint-Gobain made its most important move, disclosing that it was negotiating a merger with Pont-à-Mousson, which was closely linked with Suez Finance. This merger would create a company with annual sales across the world of approaching £1000 million, and was planned through the exchange of eleven Saint-Gobain shares for every five Pont-à-Mousson. The terms and logic of the deal were worked out by Suez. Georges Picot, the head of Suez, was reportedly furious when the news broke prematurely. Picot had been fully aware of the problems at Saint-Gobain; he thought that these pointed to a full takeover by Suez, but had hoped to avoid public embarrassment for de Vogüé by deferring the takeover until later in 1969, when de Vogüé was due to retire. But the news leaked, and in August of that year de Vogüé had the task of writing again to Saint-Gobain shareholders.

He explained that in the new merger company, to be called Saint-Gobain-Pont-à-Mousson, the Suez group would own between 14 and 15 per cent, while the company would in turn take a slightly smaller shareholding in Suez itself. The deal was certainly done in a style of which Picot approved. Perhaps he deserves the final comment, which gives the verdict of French industry on the Anglo-Saxon variety of takeover battle. He told Suez shareholders:

We consider, for our part, that matters of association such as a takeover or merger should proceed in a peaceful atmosphere between the purchaser and the company which is the object of the operation.

But Riboud, after all, won the last trick. The year after the battle, and again with the help of Lazard, he scored a major coup by taking over Société Européene de Brasseries, Europe's largest brewery, whose acquisition virtually doubled group sales. 'Growth, distribution, and European-wide size is what we've always been after,' explained Riboud. 'I can think only of expanding and now, happily, I'm off to an extremely good start.' Picot and Riboud neatly summarize the contrasting attitudes held in France towards company development.

Chemical Bank *v* Mr Steinberg

On 21 February 1969, Sir George Bolton, chairman of the powerful Bank of London and South America, and a former executive director of the Bank of England, wrote to his representative in New York:

> I do not know how the reactions of other large customers of the Chemical Bank will coincide with my own; but if a company that has recently jumped into prominence and that has no real background having really been created out of inflation were to acquire an important bank such as the Chemical, then I should at once close our account. You might mention this to Bill Renchard or whoever else you know near the top of the Bank.

Bill Renchard was the chairman of the Chemical Bank of New York and the company allegedly 'created out of inflation' was the Leasco Data Processing Equipment Corporation headed by Saul Steinberg. Leasco's attempt to take over Chemical Bank, the fifth largest bank in the US, provoked one of the outstanding examples of a financial establishment turning on and defeating an attack from outside.

Saul Steinberg, then in his early thirties, was born in Brooklyn and grew up in a middle class, Jewish environment. Young Steinberg went up to the Wharton School of Business, where he set out in a paper the two bases of his future success: the growth of data processing coupled with the use of leasing. His paper was rejected, and Steinberg went to work in his father's household goods business. In 1961, after persistent badgering, his father agreed to put up $25000 for Saul to start the Ideal Leasing Co. Saul Steinberg now set his plan in motion: to buy a computer from IBM, offer it for rental at lower rates than IBM, and depreciate over five years. The key to success was the contract with the lessee; this gave Steinberg the collateral he needed to borrow the necessary cash. In effect, Steinberg was applying to computer leasing the same notion that had made money for tanker charterers and property developers.

Steinberg signed his leasing deal with Harris Intertype in May 1961, and from then on Ideal grew fast. By August 1965, Steinberg was able to go public, and the re-named Leasco, showing revenues of more than $8 million a year and net profits of $225000, was sold on the flattering price-earnings

116

ratio of 15. Steinberg's success had been impressive, and the potential in computer leasing remained great. But from 1967 onwards, Steinberg began to diversify; his basic business, computer leasing, was subject to competition from new entrants, overall profitability rested partly on the level of interest rates, and any computer leasing concern depended essentially on the research and development plans of the manufacturer, in this case IBM. There was a financial motive too, that shares valued on a price-earnings basis of 30 to 45 (which they reached in 1967–68) could be used to buy companies that were valued on a less optimistic basis.

During 1968, therefore, Steinberg moved into Europe, paying $9 million for Inbucon which owned Associated Industrial Consultants, one of the leading British management consultants. This bid, incidentally, did not go entirely smoothly. Colin Perry, who was chief executive of the AIC company which advised on mergers, publicly opposed the bid, though without success. This was, in a sense, the prelude to what was easily Steinberg's most head-line-catching deal for the British public, his bid for Pergamon Press. The whole Leasco-Pergamon episode, which acquired notoriety in the autumn of 1969, has been thoroughly analysed in the British press. For Robert Maxwell, founder and moving spirit of Pergamon, the deal dealt some severe blows. For Saul Steinberg, all that happened helped to underpin the criticisms of Leasco that had been growing on Wall Street. But for Leasco itself, the Pergamon episode was dwarfed by the takeover of Reliance Insurance of Philadelphia and the abortive bid for Chemical Bank of New York. The first bid, which involved more than £100 million, transformed Leasco's entire operations; Steinberg's defeat over Chemical, a bank with over £3000 million worth of total assets, raised a series of questions about the direction of Leasco's company strategy.

The effect of the Reliance takeover on Leasco can be seen from a few figures. As late as August 1968, Leasco was still a relatively small operation, principally engaged in leasing computers and the provision of related services, with only 800 employees. By February 1969, after thirteen acquisitions including Reliance, it employed 8500 people and did business in fifty countries. Since 1965, when Leasco took its present name, its net income had increased from $196 000 to $43·9 million in 1969, thanks largely to Reliance. In this period its assets increased from $7·6 million to $1200 million.

On 24 June 1965, when Leasco Data Processing Equipment Corporation was incorporated in Delaware, it had just seventeen full-time employees. After the Reliance acquisition, gross total assets reached about $1000 million. No one could accuse Steinberg of keeping his plans secret. A Leasco prospectus of 30 January 1969 stated:

Leasco is actively seeking additional areas in which it can expand its business. . . . Management has also had under consideration proposals for expansion, through acquisition activities in the financial services field,

117

including banking, insurance, consumer finance, and investment management services.

'Racquel' Acquisition

On 19 March 1968, just two months before Leasco paid over $4 million for a 3 per cent stake in Reliance, an internal Leasco memo said that the 'Racquel' acquisition was being actively pursued. Racquel was the Leasco code name for Reliance, a name chosen from Racquel Welch, the curvaceous American film actress. Asked to explain his choice of code name, Steinberg later said that Reliance, like Miss Welch, was 'big and beautiful'. The attraction of Reliance to Leasco was what was known in the trade as surplus surplus. In other words, that part of Reliance's total assets in excess of what was needed to meet the needs of policy holders; estimates of the amount involved in Reliance ranged up to $125 million. The plan was to use this surplus through the vehicle of a financial services holding company, whose creation would avoid legislation which existed in some states to limit the use of insurance company assets. Steinberg announced his tender offer for Reliance on 22 June 1968 and by 14 October the takeover was complete. His bid was resisted by the directors of Reliance but their resistance ended after an improvement in Leasco's bid terms. Steinberg later explained the logic of his bid – to give Reliance shareholders a higher dividend, a preferred position in the capital structure and, above all, the growth potential of Leasco's equity.

But Steinberg had his eyes on bigger game. On 6 November 1968, barely a month after the Reliance bid, Mr Lages of the First Jersey National Bank reported his first purchase of shares in the $8967 million Chemical Bank of New York. It is not entirely clear why Leasco's attention lighted on Chemical: its growth record was not impressive, but Steinberg's eye was also caught by a circular on Chemical issued by one of the leading Wall Street specialists in bank shares, M. A. Shapiro. Over the months that followed, Leasco bought a total of 300000 shares in Chemical, perhaps $18 million worth, being careful not to register the shares in order not to alert the Chemical directors, headed by William Renchard. For several years, some 55000 shares had been owned in Reliance; Leasco bought an extra 300000.

Steinberg took elaborate precautions to keep his buying secret, notably by using the code name 'Faye' in all references inside Leasco to Chemical Bank. On his choice of code name for Chemical Bank (after using Racquel for Reliance), Steinberg disclosed that the code was chosen in honour of Faye Dunaway, who was starring in the 'thirties gangster film *Bonnie and Clyde*. (One wonders at the code name used for Pergamon . . .) But for all Steinberg's care, Bill Renchard of Chemical Bank heard rumours of a coming takeover bid that autumn. These rumours quietened down until late January

1969, when they recurred more seriously. By 31 January, Renchard had received what he called 'solid intelligence' that Leasco was interested in making a bid. Renchard was thus in the fortunate position of knowing about a likely bid from Leasco a week before this burst on the public. In takeovers, as in war, prior intelligence can be extremely useful.

Chemical's Interest

Bill Renchard did not explain how he came to know about Leasco's plans, but it is clear that Chemical Bank had been interested for some time in Leasco's affairs. As far back as December 1967, an employee of Chemical Bank, Robert Van Buren, had been assigned to follow Leasco's reported attempt to acquire Security National Bank, although Chemical explained that Van Buren was acting purely in his capacity as an assessor of future business prospects for the bank. Bill Renchard said:

> We have everything divided geographically, and certain officers are assigned to certain parts of the country and they follow everything that is in that part of the country including all the names, banks, correspondent banks, industrial, commercial prospects . . .

But even apart from Van Buren's interest, the corporate client department of Chemical Bank kept in touch with Leasco. In August 1968, Robert Lipp, vice-president of Chemical Bank, had a report prepared by the accountants, Phillips, Appel and Walden, on the accounting methods used by the Leasco Corporation. Renchard later explained that Chemical Bank was thinking of forming a holding company and, therefore, organized a study of all leasing companies against the possibility of going into the leasing business itself.

By 3 February 1969, Chemical was very much aware that Leasco was on the warpath and Robert Lipp, the vice-president, drew up a counter-plan. He listed several steps that could be taken as a defence against a proposed offer from Leasco, such as a one for one share exchange. Lipp's list of counter-measures was comprehensive and ingenious. Item number four, for example, was:

> Use of outside help – retention of the best solicitation firms both for Chemical's use and to deny these firms from the opposition. Investment banks and financial publicity firms are also helpful.

Lipp also suggested legal action to block the offer and particularly, an especially astute move, the establishment of a computer leasing subsidiary in order to present Leasco with an anti-trust problem. Lipp also proposed tendering for the stock of Leasco itself, although he conceded that Leasco's high price-earnings ratio might make this difficult.

Two days later, on 5 February, still one day before the bid became public, two more of Chemical's top executives launched an even more sophisticated plan to thwart the Leasco takeover. John Riddell, senior vice-president, wrote to Charles Eddy, executive vice-president, to report on the latest defensive ideas:

> Politically it would seem expedient to contact representatives of the Senate Banking Finance Committee and its counterpart in the House concerning this matter.

> Contact should be made at the Federal Reserve Bank here in New York as well as through Bill Martin, so that they too might be aware of the situation.

> Some discussion could also be held with the Superintendent of the banks in the state of New York.

Bill Renchard did talk to William McChesney Martin, the well known head of the Federal Reserve, eleven days after the memorandum and after Leasco had in fact decided to give up the fight, though before Leasco had publicly acknowledged defeat. Chemical had also pondered a takeover of the Security National Bank of Long Island, in a deal which would have meant that the merger group could be taken over only by another bank. The defence memorandum suggested that this Security National takeover should be highlighted, in a significant phrase, by 'particular reference being made to the need to maintain the sanctity of the banking system'. The defence scheme continued: 'The potential merger should also be explored in an effort to create a road-block in terms of the Justice Department looking into any takeover attempt by Leasco.' The Chemical Bank directors continued to believe the most obvious candidate was Aetna Life, although another major insurance company, Hartford Fire, was reckoned a likely prospect, with the backing of Bournemouth-born Harold Geneen, the chairman of International Telegraph and Telephone, which controlled Hartford.

Accountants' Advice

Bill Renchard was thus well prepared to fight off Leasco, but even these plans did not exhaust all the weapons in the Chemical Bank armoury. At the end of December 1968, Renchard asked Price Waterhouse, the eminent accountants, for a list of actions the company could take to defend itself against an unwanted takeover. Item number six in Price Waterhouse's analysis was nothing if not frank:

> Attempt to discourage the lending of funds to the potential acquirer. Through banking and other financial contacts the company officials may be able to prevent the company making the offer from obtaining sufficient funds to finance the purchase of shares tendered.

But probably Renchard's most formidable move was to make contact with his fellow banker, Donald M. Graham, the chairman of the Continental

Illinois and Trust Company of Chicago, a bank which headed a consortium of some forty institutions throughout the US, which had agreed to provide Leasco with more than $130 million of finance. Renchard tried to reach Graham on 6 February, the day the *New York Times* released the news to the public, but could not contact him until the following day when Graham and many other bankers were meeting at the Berkley Hotel in New York for a banking convention. Renchard urged Graham to discourage Leasco from its attempt to acquire Chemical Bank. One could well endorse the *New York Times*, of 6 February which carried an article stating that: 'William S. Renchard, Chairman of the Chemical Bank, sounded like a Marine Corps Colonel in presenting his battle plan for what he believes may well develop.'

A good deal of Leasco's buying was handled through Reliance Insurance Co., which at the time of its takeover held about 55 000 shares in Chemical Bank. By 31 December 1968, Reliance held more than 100 000 shares in Chemical – extra shares which would have cost Leasco about $8 million. All these purchases were made through the First Jersey National Bank and held in a nominee account. Rumours of a coming bid for Chemical multiplied, but the takeover plan hit the public through the columns of the *New York Times*, where, on 6 February, Robert Metz launched a story about Leasco's plans for a takeover. From this point onwards, for two weeks, events moved fast.

At the time of the *New York Times* article, Steinberg and Renchard had never met. The day after Metz's revelation, Renchard wrote to Steinberg:

> Rumours have come to our attention that your company may be considering an attempt to acquire control of Chemical Bank New York Trust Co. We feel it important that you be aware that our counsel's advice is that any attempt by your company to acquire control of Chemical Bank New York Trust Co. would raise serious problems under the anti-trust laws. We are in the process of completing steps to form a holding company for the announced purpose of expanding our operations in financially related areas. These areas, existing and planned, include those in which your company is operating and is a significant factor.

The General Says No

Before Steinberg could reply, Chemical had been in touch with its financial advisers. One of the Bank's first moves was to contact White Wheld, the powerful investment house, one of whose partners was a director of Leasco. Chemical Bank was assured by White Wheld that it had advised Steinberg that it would not support Leasco's attempts to acquire Chemical Bank. On the day the *New York Times* article was printed, Renchard took the major step of telephoning General Lucius Clay – a partner in Lehman Brothers, the famous banking house that advised Leasco. He asked General Clay whether Lehman knew of Leasco's plans and what its position was in respect of the planned takeover. Lehman Brothers called a meeting of the partners the following day, after which General Clay telephoned Renchard and told him Lehman Brothers had concluded that it would advise Leasco against proceeding.

All this was taking place within a few hours of publication of the *New York Times* story which, it would seem, originated with another *Times* writer Eric Heineman, who had telephoned Bill Renchard on the previous day. This was five days after Renchard had received his 'solid intelligence' that Leasco were planning a bid, and after Renchard had already made plans for battle. When approached by Heineman, Renchard could reasonably take an optimistic view. In his own words: 'I felt it was just as well if it came out in the press.'

To complete the pattern for a Marine Corps battle plan, Renchard set up a 'Chemical Bank task force' to fight off the unwanted invader. This was headed by Joseph McFadden, vice-president of special assignments. The task force, which was constituted by a memorandum on 6 February, included Robert Lipp and three other executives of Chemical Bank. This task force, which also met on the day of the *New York Times* article, called in powerful outsiders, including men from First Boston, the banking group, Hornblower Weeks, the brokers, Kuhn, Loeb, the bankers, and Carvath Corporation, a legal firm.

Not to be outdone in defensive plans of campaign, the task force drew up its own recommendations:

(*a*) Engage a powerful public relations firm;

(*b*) Consider acquiring a 'large' insurance company;

(*c*) 'There is some question about the breadth of the market on the Leasco stock, and it might be possible to attack its value if needs be';

(*d*) Consideration might well be given to looking for a rescue party. One unsolicited rescue party emerged in the form of Great Lakes Carbon, who offered to acquire a substantial amount of stock to keep it in friendly hands. Bill Renchard thanked Great Lakes Carbon directors, but declined their offer.

One intriguing example of Chemical's network of friends emerged from the Congressional inquiry. During the concern about bank mergers, Senator Sparkman was interested in bank holding companies, and was pondering whether to take action in the early part of that week. A Mr Simmons, who worked for Carvath, the legal advisers to Chemical Bank, drafted the bill for Senator Sparkman. When Simmons was asked later who had paid the bill for his work to assist Senator Sparkman, the answer was clear: Congressman Fogt: 'So it is an accurate statement to say that Chemical paid for your work on this?' Mr Simmons: 'Oh, yes.'

Some of Chemical's shareholders quickly made clear their support for the board against Leasco. Adams Express Company, which held 14 200 shares, contacted Alfred Howser, who was in charge of the bank's investment department, to say that it had been approached by two firms of brokers, Brear Stearns and Wood Struthers, to sell its shares. The company did not sell; reasonably enough, the Chemical executives stated: 'We consider the Adams people to be very friendly.' Even more prestigious was the Continental Insurance Company, which stated that it would not sell its Chemical shares, even when offered a premium of no less than $30 a share. Continental Insurance held 63 000 shares in Chemical, so that its decision to ignore a $30 premium meant that it was turning down a profit of $1·89 million. Chemical Bank was playing an extremely sophisticated game. If it had been involved in any conspiracy or 'unlawful agreed concert of action' to injure Leasco, then there would have been a violation of US legislation under the Sherman Act. Short of that, there would be no violation. Chemical was careful to ensure that its actions stopped short of that point.

Lunch with the Press

The day after Robert Metz's *New York Times* article was also an eventful one for Saul Steinberg. On that day, he had lunch with Eric Heineman, the inspirer of the revelation, a lunch which had previously been deferred; Steinberg felt that a further deferment would be ungracious. Steinberg had originally been anxious to meet Heineman, because of the latter's knowledge of banking legislation but their lunchtime conversation on 7 February turned largely on Leasco and Chemical. Heineman, it would seem, later talked to Mr Maxwell, of Chemical Bank's public relations department, who was able to gather the gist of his conversation with Steinberg. As a result of Maxwell's report, Renchard himself talked to Heineman and was able to draw up some helpful pieces of information about the battle as Steinberg saw it at that point. Renchard's notes ran as follows:

(*a*) Not sure about Chemical;
(*b*) Will first propose a friendly deal which he (Steinberg) supposed Chemical would turn down;
(*c*) Not authorized by the board to do anything;
(*d*) Don Graham has mixed feeling – high regard for Steinberg – concerned about effective banking;
(*e*) $100 million of Reliance assets are redundant.

By a happy, or unhappy, coincidence, key American bankers were assembled in New York for the Bankers' Association Trust conference. Steinberg went there to call on Don Graham, head of Continental, which was the leader in Leasco's financing group. Bill Renchard also went. 'I must have talked to 300 bankers,' he said later. Everyone wanted to talk to him about Leasco's bid, and Renchard no doubt expressed himself with vigour. Significantly, Renchard talked to some of the key banks which participated in Leasco's credit arrangements, notably United California, Wells Fargo, and First National Bank of Boston. Renchard asked Graham if he would point out to Leasco the undesirable results of an acquisition both on Chemical and on banking in general.

The following day, Saturday, 8 February, saw unaccustomed activity at Chemical's Pine Street headquarters in Wall Street. Bill Renchard called together his task force to plan a massive counter-attack to a Leasco bid. A detailed plan of campaign was drawn up. (At this stage, Leasco had not yet formally stated their intention to make a bid – much less had it launched a takeover offer.)

Cards were to be sent to all holders of 250 or more shares in Chemical and telephone groups were to be set up. An analysis was also made of nominee holders of Chemical shares, with particular reference to nomineee accounts which had increased their holdings to more than 50 000 shares between January 1968 and January 1969. The search of nominee accounts showed some interesting developments. Carothers and Clark, which held no shares on 20 January 1968, owned no less than 98 800 by 20 January 1969, and by 6 February had increased its interest to 134 400 shares. Rich and Company had bought an extra 107 500 shares during this period, while Reliance Insurance Company itself held 188 049 shares as of 6 February, and bought an extra 15 000 during that day.

The Chemical task force also took a hard look at the holders of Leasco stock, and discovered that eighteen mutual funds had no less than 27 per cent of Leasco's equity capital. Bill Renchard also talked to the New York Superintendent of Banks, Mr Willy, and to Alfred Hayes, head of the Federal Reserve Bank of New York.

Steinberg was in the position of a general who sees his adversary putting up defences and preparing a counter-attack before his own offensive can get under way. 'They are beginning to feel the pressure' was Renchard's assessment of Steinberg's feelings as expressed to Eric Heineman on 7 February. There is no doubt that the pressure continued to mount. Probably the most typical banking view was that expressed to Steinberg by Don Graham, that this merger was the correct long term trend for US banking but, that he did not approve of Leasco taking control of Chemical. According to Steinberg, Graham told him that a takeover 'would not be a good thing for banking and confidence in banking'.

Monday, 10 February, was a day of bad snow in New York and Steinberg was caught in Manhattan. Steinberg telephoned Bill Renchard, and the two agreed to meet for lunch. Renchard obligingly sent his car to collect Steinberg and the two men met for the first time.

Much of the lunch (described by Renchard as 'very pleasant') was spent in general discussion, but Steinberg made the specific undertaking that he would make no formal announcement at the Leasco shareholders meeting which was due on the following day. The two men also agreed to set up a meeting of Chemical and Leasco executives, after the Leasco shareholders' session.

Visit to Chemical

The Leasco shareholders' meeting lasted from 2.30 p.m to around 4 p.m. Steinberg, in reply to a shareholder's question, confirmed that Leasco was interested in Chemical – the first public statement from the Leasco side. That same afternoon, Steinberg, Bernard Schwartz, and other Leasco executives called at the Chemical Bank headquarters. Steinberg himself called the meeting 'cordial but not overly friendly'. Steinberg outlined Leasco's plans and explained why he thought it made sense for Leasco to have a large money base. The general drift of the meeting was that Leasco would like to move if Chemical was interested, while agreeing to talk to Chemical before planning any further action. Leasco also said, though Steinberg and Renchard seem to have somewhat differing views of the discussion, that a tender offer would be 'loathsome' but that it might have to resort to a tender in order to fulfil its aims. Renchard and his colleagues stressed the difficulties of a forced takeover and mentioned possible restrictive legislation. Rather skilfully, Chemical asked the Leasco executives for their overall 'grand scheme' if the bank was to show an interest. Leasco discussed travel agencies, financial planning, and new economic and social conditions with the accent on selling to the small investor, together with the wider spread of wealth and company ownership. Both sides appear to have agreed, which seems to represent a big concession by Steinberg, that Leasco would not take over the Chemical Bank Corporation, but that the bank should remain autonomous while a fresh subsidiary would be set up, owned fifty-fifty by the Bank and Leasco. In effect, Leasco would run Chemical's one bank holding company.

Renchard talked to Steinberg again on Friday, 14 February, and arranged to meet him the following Thursday at 9.30 a.m. In the meantime, on 12 February, the Chemical Bank executives held a further meeting. During this meeting, they produced a list of the top fifty companies for which they were transfer agents. The aim of the meeting was:

> To put down in a little more specific form or document a little more fully what we felt would be the adverse effects on the business of the Bank if an unfriendly takeover should be successful.

On 13 February, another meeting of the task force took place, including both bank executives and investment bankers. They discussed taking over a small casualty company, but they agreed that this could in no event create a major anti-trust problem for Leasco. They also considered having Hartford Fire bid for Chemical. A Bank executive suggested that they might consider another large insurance tie-up. None of these ideas, however, ever led to negotiations with any of the insurance companies. An even more crucial meeting took place the following day, when the members of the task force agreed to go ahead with the formation of a bank holding company, with all formalities completed by the following Monday, 17 February, which was still three days ahead of the meeting with Steinberg.

The task force also prepared what could well have been a crucial counter-blow, which is summed up in a brief message: 'Sign Monday, contract to acquire all the stock of Estate Bank in Suffolk county.' Bill Renchard himself set out the logic of this move:

> The purpose of acquiring a bank, a small bank which we felt could be acquired without encountering difficulties with the banking authorities, would have been to put us in the category of a registered holding company immediately rather than a one-bank holding company and thereby pre-clude anyone else other than a bank from acquiring us.

Such a deal would have represented checkmate to a bid from Leasco.

Chemical Bank was thus aiming to achieve an impregnable position by 17 February. Steinberg may well have guessed at the Chemical plan of campaign, but he had other problems to face – a drop in Leasco's share price. Leasco shares fell $29 between 3 February and 20 February, from $135 to $106, and they fell further to $99 by the end of the month. This represented a drop of another 25 per cent in barely a month, a slump which almost certainly ended any hopes Steinberg might have retained of launching an unwanted bid for Chemical. Why did the Leasco share price fall?

Conglomerates Under Fire

Wall Street as a whole was running down, but this was only a part of the answer. Two other major factors were at work. One of these was a questioning of the efficiency of conglomerates, the soundness of the paper they issued during takeovers and the scope of conglomerate bids, especially if they involved banks or insurance companies. The *Wall Street Journal* of 17 February carried a major article questioning the outlook for Leasco stock and for conglomerates in general. At the same time, the influential Congressman, Wilbur Mills, announced a proposal that would rule out some of the tax advantages to conglomerates of issuing certain types of securities in acquisitions. Though Wilbur Mills' proposal was introduced only on 24 February, a press release covering his plans appeared on 10 February, by coincidence, the same day on which Saul Steinberg had lunch with Bill Renchard. The second factor was the heavy selling of Leasco stock during February 1969. According to the American Stock Exchange, no less than 378 100 Leasco shares were sold between 3 February and 20 February. Even at the lowest price of $100 a share, that would represent some £15 million in sales of Leasco shares.

126

Chemical Bank, not surprisingly, had sold the small holding of Leasco which was owned by its personal trust department, but this accounted for a tiny proportion of the total. The Congressional inquiry into the Leasco-Chemical affair did not, regrettably, establish whether the selling of Leasco shares had been inspired by:

(*a*) A revision of ideas about conglomerates in general and Leasco in particular; or
(*b*) Particular views about a bid for Chemical Bank.

What evidence exists does suggest that revised ideas about conglomerates, and revised ideas about their future rating on Wall Street, played a major part in the selling. Thus the Putnam Growth Fund, which held 325000 Leasco shares on 1 January, had sold 200500 shares by the end of March 1969. During the same period, the Keystone Custodian Fund, which formerly held 187500 Leasco shares, disposed of its entire holding.

The week beginning Monday, 17 February saw Steinberg's plans in some disarray. He said later that he had abandoned the idea of a tender offer for Chemical (i.e., an all out takeover offer, opposed or not) after the 11 February meeting with Renchard and his colleagues. A move by Leasco would thus depend on support by Chemical. 'I did not come away with the impression that they were really in love with the idea,' admitted Steinberg.

A meeting between Leasco and Chemical was scheduled for Thursday, 20 February. Chemical had not revealed any of its counter-plans, but on 19 February the superintendent of banks added his contribution to Leasco's problems. On Wednesday, the day before the Leasco-Chemical meeting, the superintendent released a statute which in New York State would have precluded any group from buying control of a bank, defined as a 10 per cent interest or greater, without the superintendent's consent. Steinberg himself spent the Wednesday in Washington discussing with officials bank legislation and, in particular, the development of one-bank holding companies. Without doubt, Steinberg appreciated Washington's concern about these banking developments, partly on grounds of policy and partly because the one-bank holding company removed banks from Federal control.

To most people, perhaps even to Leasco itself, the Thursday meeting with Chemical was a foregone conclusion. But Steinberg went to Pine Street and put the straightforward question to Chemical – was it really interested in going forward? If there was any 'negative enthusiasm' as Steinberg called it, 'our prospects in the future were too great to merge with somebody who did not share that enthusiasm'. In Steinberg's own words, the Chemical men replied 'loud and clear and friendly' that they had negative enthusiasm. We replied, said Steinberg, that we were not going forward and we would put an end to this whole episode, this 'non-event'.

Victory Telegram

Steinberg made a public statement to the same effect, and the whole episode was over. Bill Renchard fired off a telegram of victory: 'Pleased report Leasco has announced withdrawal of plan to press for affiliation with the Chemical.' This was sent to a roll-call of the US financial and industrial establishments. Telegrams went to Henry Harris, Chairman of Harris Upham and Co.; Kenneth Black, Chairman of Home Insurance; Henry Hillman, Chairman of Pittsburg-Coke; H. L. Romnes, Chairman of American Telephone and Telegraph; Lammont Du P. Copeland, Chairman of Dupont; Grant Keehn, Chairman of Equitable Life; Irwin Miller, Chairman of Cummins Engine; Crowdus Baker, Chairman of Sears Roebuck; Robert Tyson, Chairman of the Finance Committee at US Steel; J. Wilson Newman, Chairman of the Finance Committee at Dunn and Bradstreet; William Marsh, Vice-Chairman of National Distillers; Augustus Long of Miami Florida; Lewis Seiler, Chairman of Associated Dry Goods Corporation; Vincent Learson, President of IBM; Augustine Marusi, President of Borden.

On the same day, Renchard wrote a bulletin to the Chemical offices:

Mr Saul Steinberg, chairman of the board of Leasco Data Processing Equipment Corporation, has informed us this morning that in view of the lack of enthusiasm on the part of Chemical Bank for a combination with his company, he would issue a press release this afternoon to the effect that they have no further interest in pursuing their efforts to negotiate with the Bank.

For Steinberg, there was little to do but strike tents and return home. By some irony, the Department of Justice had written to Leasco to inquire into the possible monopoly implications of a merger with Chemical Bank. On 24 February, Bernard Schwartz wrote to the Justice Department confirming that Leasco had no interest in acquiring or merging with Chemical.

Chemical Bank's resistance to Leasco ranks with Saint-Gobain in France and the Savoy Hotel episode in Britain as an example of how an establishment can fight off an unwanted intruder. Probably the most fitting comment came from Steinberg himself: 'I always knew there was an establishment. I just used to think I was part of it.'

Takeover German Style

A few days before Christmas 1968, two groups of German shareholders put their seal of approval to what was Germany's biggest ever takeover. The shareholders were those of Badische Anilin-und Soda-Fabrik AG and Wintershall AG, the occasion two extraordinary meetings called for 19 and 20 December that year. Although the deal was finally approved by a large majority of shareholders in both companies, the two meetings ventilated a spate of criticism both of BASF's takeover terms and of the Wintershall management's concern for the welfare of its shareholders.

The meetings were held over 150 miles apart and many weary shareholders and directors travelled through the night after listening to nine hours of argument from the so-called 'professional opponents' who dominated the Wintershall meeting. BASF's meeting at Ludwigshafen went more smoothly and required only four hours under the expert gavel of Badische's 'grand old man' and chairman of the board, Professor Carl Würster. However, the company president, Professor Bernhard Timm, ruefully commented 'there is obviously something wrong with our publicity'. A remark which could serve as an epitaph for the old fashioned, secretive style of company management which for many years characterized German industry. BASF had become a model of modern corporate thinking, but Wintershall and the history of its ownership and interests seemed clouded in a fog of nineteenth-century mystery. Negotiations for the takeover had dragged on for nearly a year while teams of experts struggled to place a value on Wintershall's assets.

Wintershall added to BASF what was in effect a mining conglomerate with an annual turnover of DM1500 million, two-thirds of which came from oil and natural gas wells and refineries. The other one-third of Wintershall's sales consisted of potash fertilizers of which the company mined 1 million tons (half of Germany's production) each year. Wintershall lifted more oil in Germany (14 per cent of the annual total of 1·2 million tons) than any other German owned company. Wintershall was also the largest producer of natural gas in Germany with 26 per cent of the country's total exploited reserves. It controlled over 7 per cent of the refinery capacity in Germany where it had a joint operation with Shell and Esso, mostly in Lingen (3·75 million tons) and Mannheim where it worked with Marathon (3·6 million

129

tons). The Mannheim refinery was located directly across the Rhine river from BASF's plant in Ludwigshafen and its connection to the Marseilles-Mannheim pipeline ran through BASF property.

One of Wintershall's most profitable assets was the 15 per cent interest in ARAL, Europe's largest service station chain. Wintershall sold most of its petrol and diesel fuel through ARAL's 7600 Aral stations and 3500 Gasolin stations. With a quarter of the German retail market, ARAL was the last major piece of the German retail market not under foreign control, although Mobil controlled 28 per cent of the share capital. Wintershall's potash and fertilizer holdings were also of substantial interest to BASF, as Germany's largest fertilizer producer. In addition to its extensive domestic potash mines, Wintershall had staked out profitable holdings in Canada. BASF already bought one-quarter of Wintershall's annual output of 1·3 million tons of potash, in addition to calcium chloride and calcium sulphate. Wintershall's fertilizer plants would thus give BASF a complete network of fertilizer plants extending from the North Sea to Alsace. On top of all this, a 90 per cent interest in the Guano works and a 50 per cent interest in the Gewerkschaft Victor would also represent a valuable addition to Badische's output of nitrogen. Wintershall's recently built fertilizer plant in Alsace, which it owned jointly with Pec-Rhin SA, had also been a thorn in Badische's side because of its strong competition in the South German market. The bid for Wintershall gave BASF an impregnable position in the European fertilizer market.

For Wintershall, BASF represented an attractive new parent, despite the DM150 million it had to pay in inheritance taxes. BASF had been only slightly damaged in the Second World War, and had largely escaped the deconcentration of German industry which followed. However, Wintershall's conservative traditions, along with the complexity of the business, had limited its ability to raise money from both domestic and foreign capital markets and thus to raise funds for expansion, research and development, and oil exploration. Wintershall's petrochemical capacity was high, but it required a large and assured outlet. It built up an expensive team for which it had only limited employment and Wintershall could afford to spend only between £2 million and £4·5 million per year on oil exploration. Wintershall's petrol and fertilizer products were sold under the trade marks of its partners.

Farben Sisters

BASF, the bidder, had inherited the famous IG Farben empire along with its 'Farben sisters' Farbwerke Hoechst AG and Farbenfabriken Bayer AG. One intriguing side to the Wintershall takeover was the challenge it presented to Hoechst and Bayer. That the 'big three' had been going their independent ways had long been obvious, but until Bayer and Hoechst met in head-on collision over Chemische Werke Hüls, many people believed that real competition between the three companies was unlikely. However, with the absorption of Wintershall into the BASF chemical complex, it became fully apparent that the postwar shake-down of the German chemical industry had come to an end, with three well matched chemical giants opposing each other. Each had annual sales in excess of those of its old parent company and they had gathered the remnants of the old IG Farben empire around them. Later in 1969, Hoechst struck out on an even more adventurous path, by becoming the first German group to make a takeover bid in Britain. In this case, for the Berger Jenson paint group in association with Read in opposition to Sherwin Williams of the US.

By 1967, BASF had advanced from fourteenth to tenth place in the list of German companies by turnover, and by the time of the Wintershall deal its sales were running close to £600 million a year. Completion of that deal put BASF only just behind VW and Siemens as the third largest sales group in German industry.

Badische was the raw-materials base of the old Farben empire and emerged from postwar deconcentration long on raw materials and short on manufactured products. Bayer was well established in the pharmaceutical field and soon plunged into fibres and plastics. By the early 'sixties, Hoechst was hot on its heels. Badische devoted its first twelve to fourteen years to consolidating its production of raw materials and made its first important new move only a few years before the Wintershall bid, when the group decided to build a second raw-materials base in Antwerp's petrochemical complex where it invested around £60 million.

BASF's strategy was dictated by a tightly knit team of managers, a team far smaller than those which guide the destinies of Hoechst and Bayer. The financial mentor was Dr Rolf Magener, one of IG Farben's bright young men who during the Second World War hiked over the Himalayas rather than join his colleagues in a British internment camp in India. Magener worked closely with Dr Hermann J. Abs, head of the Deutsche Bank and Germany's most prominent postwar financier, who served as both Deputy Chairman and Chairman of the BASF Supervisory Board.

BASF's Antwerp expansion was followed in quick succession by the acquisition of two of Germany's largest paint and varnish producers, Glasurite and Dr Beck. In 1966, it acquired Phrix AG, one of the country's medium sized fibre producers. Then a small pharmaceutical company, Nordmark, was added at a cost of £10 million along with a small paint concern. This latter transaction was calculated to make Badische the largest paint producer on the German market, but this plan was frustrated at the last minute by Bayer which snapped up 25 per cent of the share capital. These transactions represented a major break with a tradition inherited from the old IG Farben: never compete directly with your customers.

131

Competition between Badische and Bayer also showed that the former Farben elements were prepared to fight hard against each other.

Badische's decision to change course again by integrating backwards into Wintershall's crude oil, natural gas, and potash base, gave rise to a good deal of questioning both in stock exchange circles and among shareholders. One fear was that BASF might be forced to neglect the exploitation of its newly acquired pharmaceutical division which was expected to be highly profitable. These doubts grew because BASF's fibre subsidiary had hit financial difficulties at the time of the Wintershall takeover.

The Wintershall deal, which took effect on 1 January 1969, had been planned with a good deal of care by BASF. Along with the takeover terms of nine BASF shares for ten Wintershall shares, the bidder assured Wintershall of its corporate independence, under a so-called 'domination agreement'. A domination agreement is an aspect of German Company Law which guarantees certain rights to subsidiaries and their shareholders.

Inheritance Tangle

To many Germans, it seemed that the bid from Badische Anilin had extricated the Wintershall management from a tortuous inheritance tangle. Under the terms of the will of its founder, August Rosterg, Wintershall AG was scheduled to inherit slightly more than 50 per cent of its share capital of £17·6 million, minus voting rights, no later than 1975. Herr Rosterg made this remarkable will in the early 'forties under the pressure of wartime uncertainties and his disappointment over the childless marriage of his only son, Heinz Rosterg. Old August Rosterg, who was the tenth child of a Ruhr miner, had the great fear that ownership and control might fall into strange hands. His son Heinz agreed to waive his inheritance rights in return for an annual income of £680 000 from dividends on his father's holdings until his own death, or at the latest 1975. At that time, the Wintershall AG was scheduled to inherit its own share capital in the form of the 'cuxe', an old Hanseatic term for shares, of the interlocking holding companies which had been created to hold its share capital. These were the Gewerkschaft Wintershall and Gewerkschaft Thea which were absorbed by BASF.

But the astute August Rosterg had overlooked two possibilities: one that his son would marry again and produce heirs, the other that German Company Law might be changed in such a way as to frustrate his elaborate inheritance scheme. Both possibilities were eventually realized, and Heinz Rosterg filed a suit to have his father's will set aside, while Wintershall contested the suit in order to protect its rich inheritance. An outright bid from the outside was the only quick, simple solution.

According to rumours, Hoechst had the first option to make such a bid, and when that opportunity passed, BASF stepped in. Rumour also has it that the Quandt family, one of Germany's richest, which owns an estimated one-third of the share capital of the Gewerkschaft Thea and which was reorganizing its financial interests because of the accidental death of the head of the family, acted as an intermediary. A further, personal relationship that played an important role in Badische's bid was the close friendship between Badische's Professor Timm and the late President of Wintershall, Herr Zentgraf, which gave Professor Timm a close insight into the problems of Wintershall. The agreement which he and his fellow directors worked out with the management of Wintershall provided for the early transfer by Heinz Rosterg of his interests in the Wintershall holding companies to the Wintershall AG which in turn agreed to transfer them to BASF. For his interests, which were equivalent to slightly over 50 per cent of the share capital of the Wintershall AG, Heinz Rosterg received a settlement of £400 000 cash and twelve 'cuxe' or shares of the holding companies. These shares were presumably switched for BASF shares in the takeover ratio of ten to nine at a price of around £51 530 for each 'cuxe'.

As a result of this transaction, BASF obtained a majority interest in the Wintershall AG in October 1968. Later that year, it acquired a further 25 per cent of the share capital to ensure complete control. In all, BASF issued new stock of £16·4 million nominal with a market value of just over £80 million in order to finance the Wintershall deal. About half the new BASF stock was traded for the 50 per cent of the Wintershall AG stock scattered in small lots, and the rest was used to gather in the holding company shares transferred to Wintershall AG by Heinz Rosterg.

Bidder's Confidence

Wintershall represented a sizeable new acquisition even for a group of BASF's size, but the bidder's directors exuded confidence. The Badische President, Bernhard Timm, claimed:

> We already know a little about the oil industry. Running an oil company from production through refining to the final preparation of finished petroleum products – our petrochemical raw materials – will teach us a lot about how oil costs are built, help us to order our plants from the constructors to produce exactly what we want, and enable us to squeeze the last pfennig out of each production step. As 'insiders' in oil we will be in a good position to bargain and trade with our present suppliers. We will be able to take maximum advantage of the shifts in refining that I believe are coming: it will be possible to pull ever more of one specific product out of crude in the future.
>
> Our kind of technical finesse becomes ever more important as the single steps of each chemical process are handled by more massive units instead of many small ones, as in the past. One huge unit is more efficient, but if you can't run it right your whole production falls on its nose, we in the chemical industry are more interested in this kind of finesse than the oil

133

people. With all their millions they are often stingy on the kind of research we do trying to improve each step of the process. BASF has a lot to learn in the oil industry, and we will be teaching some things, too.

BASF-Wintershall is the kind of co-operation we like, working together in a field where we can both learn. In general BASF is against the kind of co-operation where many firms pool diverse interests and very little capital. We shall wait and see whether a German oil exploration company will be practicable. For the present we can give Wintershall the kind of capital mobility they didn't have under the oil mining company holding system, and pull them with us into the dynamic of the future. Whether that means looking for oil abroad, and in what kind of co-operative form, we have not yet decided.

Professor Timm's confident approach to Badische's move into the oil industry also included the tacit admission of the pricing problems which this company faces in its battle with big international oil suppliers. BASF, like Hoechst and Bayer, had chosen independence in the procurement of oil supplies. It played off suppliers against each other in an effort to obtain the best prices, a system which worked well even during the 1967 Middle East crisis. Each company had a close link with a major international oil company: Bayer and BP had joint petrochemical co-operation, Erdölchemie; Hoechst had a major ethylene and acetylene tie-up with Marathon; and BASF owned Rheinische Olefin jointly with Shell.

When it bought Wintershall, BASF emphasized that it had no intention of altering its supply arrangements with Shell. Following the bid, BASF planned that only 10 per cent of the $100 to $115 million a year which it spent on petrochemical raw materials would go to Wintershall. Wintershall owned only one small foreign field and BASF had no plans for expanding output or rushing into exploration. Professor Timm said:

We don't want to sit on one horse and we like being able to buy cheaply on the free market. Wintershall's 1 million tons of – expensive – German oil offer us some of the fractions we need, but Wintershall has no tankers to bring crude to us. We depend for security on our Shell contracts.

To a certain extent, the oil procurement policy of the German chemical industry reflected the indifference which the German Government displayed towards both the independence of the German oil industry and the energy and petrochemical supply needs of the chemical sector. Coal, after all, occupied a key position in Germany both for legislators and the general public. The vote of the coalminers was still a determining factor in and election in North Rhine-Westphalia, Germany's most populous state. Any for the German public, coal and steel remained the undisputed monarchs of industry. For this reason the ailing coal industry was bolstered by elaborate and expensive multiple-aid programmes from the late 'fifties onwards. Oil, on the other hand, had been left to shift for itself with the exception of one modest grant for foreign exploration.

Oil Infant

Rather surprisingly, the oil industry had never pulled much weight in the German hierarchy. Before the Second World War, it was an infant industry and during the war it was nationalized. The international majors, who had small subsidiaries in Germany, were pushed out and the domestic companies experimented with making oil from coal. After the war, they were prohibited from continuing this process and were cut off from their Eastern European crude sources. The resources of the German oil companies were too limited for them to engage in foreign exploration and they were encouraged by government tax policies to exploit Germany's own meagre and expensive natural assets. Moreover, the German oil companies were often diversified owning big coal holdings which they were more interested in exploiting as long as they were profitable. This left a vacuum which the big international companies filled with alacrity when German oil consumption began to grow in the late 'fifties.

Oil consumption increased nine-fold from 9·1 million tons per year to 81·5 million tons between the late 'fifties and 'sixties, while the German owned refining capacity lagged sadly behind. At the time of BASF's bid, domestic companies supplied only 28 million tons of the 109 million tons of refining capacity available in the Federal Republic, and they produced only 7 million tons of crude in their German fields. Their combined annual turnover was just under £4000 million, yet they were forced to buy over 90 per cent of the crude oil they refined from foreign companies.

The international majors, on the other hand, invested an average of £120 million annually in Germany. Moreover, price competition on the international market forced the majors to supply oil to Germany at cheap prices. Germany thus gained both a major capital inflow, useful foreign know how, and a low price for a key industrial material – all of which helps to explain the cool policy towards the domestic industry adopted by the *laissez-faire* Erhard administration.

Local rivalries also contributed to the erratic career of the German oil industry. Bavaria, which was restricted to a more or less agricultural fate by the high cost of Ruhr coal, induced the international majors, by advantageous tax and local development policies, to set up an extensive refinery complex around Munich. The Trans-Alpine oil pipeline, built by ENI with Bavarian assistance, inspired a second international consortium to bring another pipeline through the Alps.

The moment of truth dawned for the German public in 1965 when the Gelsenkirchener Bergwerks AG, better known as GBAG or Gelsenberg, began the tortuous renegotiation of its fifty-year crude supply contracts with

135

Mobil Oil. In the midst of this deal, Deutsche Erdöl, Germany's biggest oil refiner and producer, ran into financial trouble because of a protracted heating-oil war on the German market and was bought up by Texaco the following year. The DE-Texaco transaction became a political controversy which contributed to the fall of the Erhard administration, after the government had first blocked the deal and then acquiesced because of the cost of financing DE. The GBAG-Mobil Oil dispute came to an amicable end (thanks partly to the efforts of City banker Sir Siegmund Warburg), but the German public had awakened to the fact that nearly 75 per cent of its oil industry had passed into foreign hands.

The international majors followed a discreet policy in Germany, by co-operating closely with a government sponsored programme of 'self-limitation' of the expansion of refinery capacity. In the last resort, they faced the possible threat of import licences and taxes if they did not co-operate. But some German critics of the 'self-limitation' system saw it as a government sponsored cartel which offered many advantages to the internationals, who were responsible for a series of price wars on the heating-oil and petrol market. These wars kept prices low, but also brought many small companies into financial difficulties.

French Bid Vetoed

All this helps to explain the unprecedented refusal by Germany to allow Compagnie Française des Pétroles to buy some 40 per cent of the shares of the Gelsenkirchener Bergwerks AG (GBAG). This resulted in a flat rejection of the deal by the Minister of Economics, Karl Schiller. CFP, while a publicly quoted oil company, has the French State as its largest single shareholder. The fact that the Federal Government felt that the retention of GBAG in German hands was of sufficient importance in face of its EEC commitments is indicative of the serious view which the government took of the future energy needs of the country – and the pressing need to co-ordinate the conflicting energy policies of the EEC countries. The German rejection of the CFP bid for GBAG was the forerunner of the French refusal to allow Fiat to bid for complete control of Citroen: both these moves represented severe blows against European company integration. Professor Schiller took care to emphasize, however, that the German Government did not object to CFP's participation in the German oil industry as such.

Following Badische's bid for Wintershall, the much neglected development of long term plans for Germany's energy needs got under way, beginning with the transfer of ownership of around 80 per cent of the country's coalpits to a private holding and operating company. Almost before this company had made its debut, the new German Oil Company was founded. The establishment of such a company, which had been under discussion for three years, was not possible until the Coal Holding Company had been formed, because Germany's major oil producers and refiners were still 'composites' with coalpits which were a drag on their profitability.

The all German oil company was hardly the massive undertaking which had originally been planned. Its activities were initially confined to a joint crude oil supply organization. In addition to GBAG and VEBA, a 50 per cent government holding company, the members included Saarbergwerke, Preussag AG, Wintershall AG, Union Wesseling, Deilmann Bergbau, and Deutsche Schachtbau. Together, these firms accounted for some 35 per cent of the sales of crude oil in Germany and controlled around 29 per cent of the available refinery capacity. They thus constituted the 'blocking minority' in the German oil industry which the then Minister of Economics, Professor Schiller, believed was essential in order to preserve Germany's independence in this field. They also sold around 20 per cent of all the petrol bought by German drivers, as well as controlling a substantial share of the capital in Aral AG. Of great long term importance was their 30 to 40 per cent share of the natural gas business in Germany. The long term problem for this group will be to secure adequate foreign crude oil reserves. (Only GBAG has a substantial interest in foreign fields, as the result of its partnership with Mobil Oil in Libya.) The new crude oil supply company was given a share capital of DM50 million and received loans from the Federal Government of up to about £12·4 million per year for exploration. It also received tax concessions and special depreciation priviieges. The government held no direct financial interest in the company; but as majority owner of VEBA, Preussag, and Deutsche Schachtbau, the government clearly possessed a big indirect influence.

As the new owner of Wintershall, BASF pulls substantial weight in this organization where it is by far the largest and financially most powerful company. It is thus possible that at long last the German oil industry has a spokesman at the centre of decisions that affect its vital interests. Each of the 'big three' had uttered vague threats at various times about moving out of the country – presumably to Antwerp where Bayer and BASF have large plants, and Flushing where Hoechst has installed itself – if more sympathetic attention were not given to their energy and petrochemical supply needs. Each also had plans for atomic power plants and had been organizing natural gas deals – but such alternatives must lie far in the future.

Printed by Cox & Wyman Ltd, London, Fakenham and Reading